Amidst lifes darkness
Choose the light ---

Howard

Chad

BLIND VISION

Howard Myers
&
Chad Myers

First Edition: March 2018

Printed in the United States of America

ISBN: 978-1-939237-57-6

Published by Suncoast Digital Press, Inc.

Sarasota, Florida, USA

DEDICATION

I dedicate this book to my wife, children and grandchildren, and to all families in the Armed Forces, whether you served in wartime or peace. May all of you enjoy the peace of mind knowing your sacrifices and commitment provide the United States with the greatest freedoms in the world.

Howard Myers

For you, the person who is willing to let go of being a victim of life, and has the courage to advance confidently in the direction of your dreams.

Chad Myers

Contents

FOREWORD

Jennie Harland-Khan

Personal Transformational Coach and Author

Have you ever noticed how some people seem to be able to bounce back from adversity, tap into resiliency and thrive, while others seem to struggle to only merely survive? Whether or not you have ever had to face the question of which response is in your character make-up, you can learn a lot from Howard Myers, a person who clearly chose to thrive and live a successful, meaningful life in spite of the most challenging of hardships.

Blind Vision is Howard Myers' story, written through his son, Chad. It is more than a memoir, it is a challenge to all, grounded in proven principles—a challenge to accept life's setbacks and traumas as what happened, not what dictates and defines who you are. Howard has quite a story to illustrate this message. It is the story of a young soldier who tragically hit a landmine in Viet Nam, rendering him totally blind and jobless, with a young family to support.

Blind Vision is the story of how Howard, despite all the odds, launched himself into a journey of self-discovery that has enabled him to experience just how magnificent he truly is. His life is dedicated to helping others find their own hope, resiliency, and magnificence, regardless of the circumstances.

I share Howard and Chad's passion for empowering others. In 2009, I made a life changing decision based on a hunch that appeared to come from nowhere. That decision had me tearfully wrenching myself away from my two young children, temporarily, to embark on a journey that would drastically reshape the entire direction of my future.

I flew from London, England, to West Palm Beach, Florida, and stepped into a personal development certification course with one of the leaders of the industry. I was terrified, questioning what on earth had brought me there.

Then, from across the room, I heard a voice I recognized—a voice with confidence, passion and curiosity that I had heard a few times on the course training calls prior to arriving at the live event.

I recalled his name...Chad. Chad Myers. Out of the 100 global trainee consultants, Chad was the one that had stood out for me. He had taken an unprecedented amount of action already as a completely new coach, willing to test everything he was learning with whomever would listen. That included his students that he taught at school, corporate leaders he was coaching, and he had boldly spent time sharing his wisdom with those who were prison inmates.

Meanwhile, I was tentatively dipping my toe in the water. I recall several times wondering where his courage had come from. Was it a learnt thing? Would I too one day dare to share, coach, and teach with such conviction?

As I write this today, I now have the answers.

It turns out that same courage lay deep inside me. I now have the deep privilege of working as a personal, transformational coach to some of the highest performers around the globe. It has taken courage, vulnerability, tenacity and resilience.

As for Chad, I have witnessed him continue on his path as a progressive educator, a powerful speaker, coach, and an insatiable student of the human mind. He reminds me of Robin Williams' character in *Dead Poets Society*, a teacher who constantly challenged and inspired others to make their lives extraordinary.

Chad's secret weapon has now been revealed to all in *Blind Vision*. If there was ever a case study of resilience, tenacity, courage and self-empowerment, then his father, Howard Myers, is it.

To answer my former question to myself, at this juncture it would be easy to conclude that Chad has the resilience, tenacity and courage that he does, because he grew up with his father as a role model.

Yet through my work as a transformational coach with a behind-the-scenes insight into the lives of exceptional high achievers, many of whom have experienced some form of trauma, or life altering hardship, I have come to understand that Howard's story, as extraordinary and inspiring as it is, is in fact a beacon of light that shines on what every single one of us has available to us. Chad has simply had the gift of seeing this first-hand, in action, in every dimension of real life.

This is what makes this book essential reading for all of us, regardless of circumstance.

As human beings we come into this world equipped with innate drivers to navigate this thing called life. From unlimited creativity to resilience, curiosity to connection, these drivers reside deep within us, available at any given moment to create and live an extraordinary life. For many, the depth and potential of these gifts are rarely realized as they walk through life with the purpose of simply getting through and surviving.

Howard Myers is not one of those people. His open-hearted story of struggle, humility, strength and self-empowerment captures the very essence of what it is to be human, and just what is possible when a decision is made to shift from victim to co-creator.

After reading this influential and important work by father and son, I'm left humbled, inspired, and more importantly, clearer than ever on my own ability to grow, impact others, and contribute in this world simply because I am a human being.

For this I am deeply grateful to Howard for having lived his life the way he has, and to Chad for the commitment it has taken to share this important message with the world.

May you, too, be touched by his story and more importantly gain an insight into what is available to you in any given moment.

"I may have lost my sight, but I never lost my vision."

—*Howard L. Myers*

PREFACE

I am an ordinary man who has had some extraordinary experiences. In particular, my life changed forever when, as a soldier in Vietnam in 1967, I lost my eyesight. Permanently. Now it is the 50th anniversary of that event, and these past five decades have been both the most challenging and the most rewarding imaginable.

For anyone who has experienced any kind of life-altering trauma like me, I'm sharing my story here. Not because it is the most amazing story you'll ever hear, but because it is one of triumph over tragedy, and people tell me it is inspiring, it is empowering, it gives hope. To my readers who are veterans: I am a veteran. If I can make a difference and help my Veteran Brothers and Sisters move from tragedy to triumph, that would be meaningful and rewarding to me.

I know many non-veterans who have heavy crosses to bear, who have had terribly unfortunate things happen that confirm, beyond a shadow of a doubt, that life is not fair. I write this with you in my heart.

A blind person asked St. Anthony, "Can there be anything worse than losing eyesight?" He replied, "Yes, losing your vision." If you or someone you know has lost their vision for a bright future, I promise you it is not too late to build a life you love—starting from wherever you are now.

You may be reading this book because you are a member of a club one never wants to join, a club comprised of people who have survived a traumatic or catastrophic event. If "triumph over tragedy" seems like a nice idea, but hardly attainable given what you have been through, then this book is for you. Throughout the dark hours of my days and nights, I've never lost my vision of having a life worth living, connected with loved ones, doing meaningful work, and most importantly, contributing to others. Whatever your vision, you can live it and it will sustain you.

In partnership with my son, Chad Myers, I have been able to share my story with many audiences. With my story of victory over victimhood, along with Chad's insight and life coaching mastery, we make an impact everywhere we go—in schools, veterans' organizations, churches and corporations. I write this not as a glowing review for myself, but as the miracle that it is.

That I could reach out and touch other people whose pain is no less than mine, who are hungry for hope and a vision of a life restored to joy…that is a miracle. I may not have the honor of meeting you in person, of sitting down in front of my glowing fireplace on a crisp Michigan evening, so I am writing this book as my way of chatting with you, in hopes you can relate, be inspired, and find yourself a little stronger. With a more firm footing, you can continue your path of healing and strengthening. This book is for anyone in "the club" of trauma survivors who could use some inspiration, a little humor, and plenty of encouragement—and certainly for those close to them who seek a greater understanding.

Howard Myers

"In World War One, they called it shell shock.
Second time around, they called it battle fatigue.
After Nam, it was post-traumatic stress disorder."

—*Jan Karon*

Chapter 1
Nam

I remember the day of April 26, 1967, as if it were yesterday. I had been sent to Vietnam as a young soldier to fight in a war. I had no idea what I was fighting for or who the enemy was.

I stepped off the plane into the hot, humid, strange country but had no time to explore or even adjust to my unfamiliar surroundings before I was loaded onto a transport truck and sent to our base camp. I found myself roaming about, talking to the other soldiers as we awaited our assignments. Finally, I was assigned to the 1st Battalion Mechanized Unit, 5th Regiment, 25th Infantry Division.

I was being sent to Cu Chi, Vietnam, about 20 miles northwest of Saigon. I was not aware of it at the time, but I was going to be part of the Reactionary Unit for the War Zones C and D. In other words, I'd been assigned to the "Lewis and Clark" division of the Vietnam War—search unfamiliar and dangerous territory, but to destroy rather than explore.

Charlie, as we called the enemy, was all over Cu Chi. It was a free-fire zone—the most bombed, shelled, gassed, defoliated, and devastated area in the history of warfare. Our company was surrounded on all sides by dangerous areas of forests and jungles. If I was looking for a way out, all I'd find was the Devil's Back Yard, also known as Hell's Half Acre, a peanut field hiding hundreds of enemy-infested tunnels beneath.

Howard, second day in Nam (March, 1967)

When I was dropped off to my company, it was the middle of the afternoon. I discovered I was the only soldier in the hooch. I started snooping around, desperately seeking a place to lay my weary head. I just wanted to sleep and escape the anxiety that had become a permanent part of my waking experience. Our headquarters in Cu Chi were rudimentary—thatched, makeshift huts were peppered throughout the base camp. There was very little vegetation inside of the camp—just dirt, mud, sandbags, military vehicles, and rows of huts. My new home in the middle of this strange country was neither comforting nor safe.

I found our company's sleeping quarters and, rather like Goldilocks, I climbed into the first empty bed I found. Exhausted from the humidity and the long drive, I tried to sleep but could not relax. Instead, I retreated into my head, playing out various terrifying scenarios. Of course I was full of stress, anxiety, and fear. I could only imagine what dreadful events were in store for me.

I was startled out of my apprehensive thoughts by a hulking, burly-bearded soldier with an unruly stench. He towered over me and began yelling about "shamming." I had no idea what he was talking about and I didn't dare ask him any questions; I just listened passively to his ugly ranting. The next day I found out he was being court-martialed for running out on the company and not fighting. As a result, he was being sent back to the States. Shamming, it turned out, was avoiding orders and slacking. I'll never forget his last words to me: "If you want to stay alive, you'll learn how to sham, soldier boy." As much as I may have been tempted at times, I just didn't have it in me to sham.

Despite my fears, and the warnings of the court-martialed soldier, I felt as if I was in the middle of the greatest party ever when my company returned to base the next morning. Awakened by the welcome sounds of music, voices, and vehicles, I ran to the door and saw soldiers of all sorts pouring into the camp. Since I'd slept in my fatigues, I walked out and started asking, "What's going on?" while more and more soldiers flocked into the barracks and began shedding their military garb for civilian attire.

It wasn't long before a few of the guys started dragging out trash cans and filling them with ice and beer. Loud music erupted from speakers I hadn't even noticed when I first arrived. Tunes by the Doors, Sonny & Cher, and the Rolling Stones began echoing throughout the camp. My new brothers were most definitely ready for a party.

They played cards or sat in small groups and gabbed, just happy to be alive. Some guys asked me to pass out the beer. *This is not too bad*, I thought. It was a far cry from the scenarios I'd been imagining all alone on my bunk. I started to feel like a bartender at the biggest party I'd ever attended. As each soldier approached me, I'd hand him a Budweiser and then reward myself with one of my own. Armed with liquid courage, I started asking questions to help me understand my new assignment and what being in Vietnam was really all about.

About four or five hours later, however, the party fizzled out. Everyone started retreating to their bunks. I finally learned where I was supposed to sleep, and I drunkenly made my way back to my hooch. One lucid thought occurred to me: *What if we're ambushed right now?* But I was too drunk to ponder this possibility for long. When I awoke, bleary-eyed and fuzzy-tongued, reality set back in. I lay in my bunk, miserable with a hangover and longing for home, wondering what would happen next.

***

A country boy from Michigan, I was slowly making the adjustment to living halfway across the planet. I remember walking about the base camp, waiting and waiting. Nothing transpired for days. I wrote letters to my wife back home and sent her my combat pay. One day a young Vietnamese girl wandered into the camp, a sweet smile on her face. I smiled back. We tried to communicate, but the language barrier prevented any meaningful conversation. She walked with me as I dropped a letter to my wife at the base camp post office. We went to the commons and ate a meal together but mostly sat in silence. This was about the extent of my interaction with the locals.

Even things that should have seemed familiar were not—
everything was surreal. American soldiers walked around like
proud hunter/warriors, some with human ears adorning their belts.
When I asked one soldier what was dangling from his belt, he said,
"These are trophies from my enemy kills!" I remember thinking,
*That's barbaric! Will I ever feel like lopping off a Charlie's ear to
decorate my belt?* It was not anything I could imagine.

In time, I was assigned to a listening post. My task was to sit
silently for most of the night in one of the nearby rice paddies and
alert the base if I heard anything suspicious. New guys were sent
to the listening posts. They were an early warning system for the
platoon, but I soon felt more like a tethered goat—expendable,
bait for the enemy.

As I prepared for the post, I took one of my dog tags and put it
in my boot, leaving the other around my neck. Then I jumped up
and down, making sure nothing rattled to give my location away.
I filled my canteen to the top to prevent any sloshing sounds. Then
I applied camo makeup to cover my face.

I did not trust the others on the night watch, and sure enough,
they fell asleep during their posts, so I ended up sitting through
two watches. What was most difficult was how my imagination
played tricks on me as I strained to hear the Viet Cong (VC)
among all the strange noises of the jungle. My hyper-vigilance
created in me a nightmarish state of confusion and fear. I had been
informed that one of the favorite tactics of the VC was to sneak
up and reverse the claymore mines, aiming them toward us, so
I had to listen hard for this kind of activity. The enemy thrived at
night and used it as their greatest weapon. Total silence was my
best protection—no eating, smoking, or talking. And certainly
no taking a leak.

The Standard Operating Procedure had been explained to me
for using the radio: two clicks on the mic once I was in position,
one click each hour after. If I saw any enemy activity, I was to
alert the platoon with repeated double-clicks on the mic while
throwing every grenade I had, then hauling up to the perimeter,

igniting pop flares to blind the enemy and give our guys a way to see what was coming.

I felt like a sitting duck. It was monsoon season, and I sat in the dark with only my poncho, my M16, and a few hand grenades. It rained all night long, and I never slept a wink. When morning finally arrived, I waddled back to camp in my soaking fatigues, changed into dry clothes, and propped up my vanity mirror to shave. I stared into the mirror. Looking back at me was the haunted face of a young man with a brown tan, bald head, and sleep-deprived baby blues.

Little did I know that this would be the last time I would ever see my reflection.

***

Just over a week after I had arrived at base camp, and only 30 days after I'd arrived in Vietnam, my unit was assigned to a 70-day search and destroy mission. I packed everything I owned into a small duffel bag, including a picture of my wife, Kristi, and we headed out.

The war in Vietnam was just getting started for me and it offered challenges that I had never encountered before. The heavy rains beat against us and our effectiveness was undermined by the brutal conditions. Not only did the army as a whole have to adapt their equipment and tactics to the terrain we encountered in the foothills of the central highlands, so did each GI. For most of us, this was our first time out of the States, the first time more than a car ride away from home. This was nothing—and I mean nothing—like Alabama, California, Kentucky, Michigan, or any place my new buddies and I had experienced before.

The land ranged from impenetrable jungles in the west to the rice paddies in the south and north. The roads were muddy quagmires demonstrating a need for constant vigilance against getting one's vehicle bogged down. The (now iconic) M113 armored personnel carrier we used could easily fall into the clutches of the rain-soaked roads.

It was the beginning of the monsoon season which added to the already miserable conditions. We were subjected to downpours of heavy, relentless rains as we traipsed through the thick sharp vines and foliage of the jungle. Struggling up and down the steep and unforgiving rises and ditches, we were greeted by massive swarms of mosquitos, leeches, ticks and fire ants. We were almost constantly drenched with water or sweat. It quite often became too difficult to bear. The ground was so wet it seemed as if it could reach up and pull the boots right off our feet.

I had only recently come out of ambush school where they teach what the enemy is about. I was still pretty green, but it took an alarmingly short period of time for me to stop thinking of the North Vietnamese as people. The VC were THE ENEMY. My mission was to SEARCH and DESTROY. For this mission, I was given an M16 rifle and ammunition as well as a few hand grenades. We were directed to drop the grenades into any wells we found as we searched the villages. I soon found it fun to drop the hand grenades into the wells and watch the water spout out the top as the grenade detonated.

Because we had to keep a daily body count, we listened for sounds of life—or rather, sounds of death—after each explosion. It began to feel like a game to me: *Kill the gooks. Kill the enemy. I want body count.* I did not realize that I was becoming a master at disassociating my emotional experiences with people. I was there to do a job, and that was it. I did not allow myself to feel any positive emotions—just anger and fear—because those intensely negative emotions made for a hell of a soldier. I recalled the chant we were taught during basic training: "I want to go to Vietnam. I want to kill a Vietcong. KILL. KILL. KILL."

I was the lead track in our company. My job was to walk alongside the armored personnel carrier as we searched various villages and traversed through the jungle. As I walked along, it occurred to me that we were no different than a gang of armed thugs intruding on an enemy's home turf, waltzing into their territory with our middle fingers straight up in the air, essentially shouting, "Yeah, I'm here in your 'hood. What are you gonna do about it?"

As we approached a new village and began asking for IDs, I saw a shirtless elderly momma san squatting to relieve herself. She grinned at us as black juice (betel leaves with areca nuts and tobacco that she chewed for a high) trickled down her neck, matching her greasy black hair and black pajama bottoms. I remember thinking, *Myers, this is not something you want to remember.* I did not know it at the time, but this would be my last visual image of a female.

This particular day, as we stood in front of a hooch, my sergeant, Zigferd Jannitta, handed me a flashlight and .45 pistol. "Myers! Crawl into this tunnel to see if there's anyone down there," he barked in his Staten Island accent.

"You're shitting me?" I asked, sure it was a joke. They wouldn't send a person into a dark tunnel.

"No, I am NOT shitting you!" he said, totally serious. "Someone's got to do it."

Being the new guy on the block, that someone was me. "Get down there now and see if there's some VC hiding in there!" he barked again.

I dropped my pack and lay on my belly. The opening was only about two feet wide, as most of the Vietnamese were smaller-framed than Americans. White terror came over me as I started wriggling down into the darkness. I thrust myself deeper into the tunnel, sure that at any moment tragedy would strike. *Is this the day I die?*

We did not know it at the time, but the entire Cu Chi base, a 1,500-acre complex housing 4,500 men, was situated directly over a thriving rat's nest of VC tunnels. The VC knew these tunnels were a thorn in our sides. Some of these tunnels were elaborate, with cleverly hidden trap doors. Some zigzagged up, down, and sideways as far as 18 feet into the earth.

I cannot express how glad I was to find there was no one down there.

A day later, Sergeant Jannitta came over to where I was sitting. "Myers, have you ever fired a 50 caliber machine gun?" he asked, his New York accent so very out of place in the jungles of Vietnam.

"Sir, yes sir!" I proudly asserted.

The soldier assigned to our personnel carrier no longer wanted this duty, so I was assigned to a new position as a 50 caliber machine-gunner on our armored personnel carrier that was loaded with mines, C4 explosives, and hand grenades. I thought that this would be much better than being lead track, but it was in no way as glamorous as I'd imagined. It just made me more of a target.

I remember receiving the radio directives from the lieutenant in the rear. He was frustrated because I could not understand his orders. I yelled out to my sergeant, "You may want to get up here and talk to the lieutenant." We had just pulled out of one of the jungles as Sergeant Jannitta jumped on the radio. Our orders were to head northwest.

***

We don't know what we have until it is gone. Sunsets melting over the horizon, white caps on Lake Michigan, the grinning faces of your family—vivid images of life that we all take for granted. I had 20/20 vision when I arrived in that hot, humid country full of lush green trees and blooming foliage. I just didn't know how little time I had left to appreciate it all.

It was yet another oppressively hot day in monsoon season as we headed northwest. We were just coming out of the jungle. I used my machete to cut some pineapples out of a tree. My gun hit a red ant nest, and I removed my steel pot helmet to swat them away. Our jeep driver was looking for a shaded area so we could enjoy a few moments to eat lunch.

As we rolled toward the trees, a memory from ambush school flitted through my mind: never pull into shaded areas, a common place for the enemy to plant landmines.

"Lonnie," I said, "don't pull in between those trees! There could be a—"

BOOM!

The lights went out. My life, as I knew it, was over.

"Trauma creates one of four types of people: victims, rescuers, or perps—or if you are really lucky and really strong and very willing and brave, survivors."

—*Allison Anders*

Chapter 2
Trauma Begets Trauma, Hope Begets Hope

On Tuesday, February 26, 1946, in Thomasville, North Carolina, my biological father, Howard Myers, Sr., awoke on a cold morning to attend to his bicycle shop. A 17-year-old attempting to transition into manhood, he and his 16-year-old wife, Louise, were parents to one- and-a-half-year-old Fred and their soon to be born second son—me, five months from my birth.

As my father approached the old building that housed his dream bicycle shop, he made a grave mistake. Instead of grabbing the can of kerosene to light his fire to warm the shop, he picked up the one filled with gasoline. Instantly, the small shop burst into flames. My father ran out of the building and rolled around on the ground to smother the flames which had engulfed his young frame. His parents rushed him to the Thomasville Hospital, while my mother was left home to take care of my toddler brother.

The terribly burned seventeen-year-old father and husband fought for his life as long as he could. Hours later, he took his last breath, but not before he murmured to his parents, "Promise me you will be good to Louise." He never said goodbye to his wife and son. On February 27, 1946, Howard Sr. passed away, leaving a sixteen-year-old widow with one son and another on the way. That

11

unborn child was me. A pattern of tragedy, of trauma, was being laid down in my life, even before I was physically present. More trauma transpired following this tragedy. No time was allowed for mourning, grieving, or healing. None. My grandparents, Gurney and Effie Myers, refused to allow my mother to visit the hospital. She was not allowed to say goodbye to her first love, her husband, her children's father.

One year before Howard's birth, Howard Myers, Sr. (1945)

No one really knows the motive behind not allowing my mother to visit Howard, but she was to endure even more hardship as she lived with her deceased husband's parents who became bitter over their son's tragic death. My mother wanted to provide a safe environment to help us grow up and lead happy lives, but she was a minor and, as such, became trapped in their dark world. My grandparents seemed to be engulfed in a world of fear, full of desperate attempts at control. They had been overly protective of their only son, treating him like a child even as he grew past puberty. They did not want him to date anyone and tried to keep him home, away from friends, especially girls. In their eyes, no one was good enough for their son and they watched over him in every way. Eventually he dropped out of school, married and became a young father. Despite their hovering, control and anxiety, they could not prevent a terrible accident nor save their precious son's life.

Many lack the knowledge of how to heal from trauma and are unaware of the effects of trauma to the brain and heart. Many become victims of their circumstances and upbringings. Clearly, my grandfather did not adhere to his son's final request to "be good to Louise." He fell into the trap of trauma, becoming bitter and angry over my father's death. Is it possible he blamed my mother...maybe he blamed himself?

When my mother wanted to apply for Social Security, my grandparents prohibited her from doing so. Instead, they insisted that she leave the house to find work to provide for her boys. She later told stories describing how this time was a living hell for her.

How did she get involved in such a family? She had fallen in love with my father, who was described as a positive, easy-going, godly man. My grandfather would have none of this youthful romance. He forbad them to see each other (evidently, he had never read Romeo and Juliet), thus prompting 15-year-old Howard and 14-year-old Louise to run away and get married so they could be together. By all accounts, my grandfather was a mean man. He could be very sarcastic and always wanted everything his way.

When my mother was forced to live with Howard's parents, his father was controlling and at times physically abusive. Once, he slapped her to the floor while she was still pregnant with me.

Once I had arrived, my grandfather's rancor remained directed at my mother. My grandparents followed my mother around and totally invaded her life. Her in-laws undid nearly everything that she did for my brother and me. They were very set in their ways and showed no regard for my mother's role as our mom. In a very short time, mom became quite bitter at life and began asking hard questions such as, "How could God take away my husband and leave me with two small children?" If that wasn't enough to bear, she also had to live under the iron rule of her in-laws. She was even prohibited from seeing her own parents even though they lived nearby.

As time passed, word about my mother's circumstances traveled around Thomasville and one courageous preacher knocked at the Myers' residence to share his concerns about the family and the young children. This only infuriated my grandparents and seemed to force them to take drastic measures to "protect their grandchildren." Once the preacher departed, they left the house to go and speak to an attorney about taking custody of my brother and me, away from our mother. What amazes me about my mother is the fact she was so young, yet so responsible as a mother. Her only desire was to have us boys into a safe, loving environment. It was clear Gurney wanted control and would use nearly any means possible to have things his way. For whatever reason, he wanted to gain custody of my brother and me. My mother thought differently. She was adamant that no one would take her young children away from her.

Our mom had one ally, Jimmy—my grandfather's father—who lived in a shack at the back of the property. For some time, she had been secretly meeting him and they were plotting her escape. With my grandparents actually visiting an attorney, my mother realized that she needed to take action; now was the time to take the leap into the unknown and leave her living hell. With Jimmy's help, she gathered up my brother and me and ran off into the woods. She carried me on her hip, and Freddie ran alongside our great-grandfather, traveling through the woods as quickly as we could. She used the fear of her in-laws returning to fuel her every step. Her only goal was to get from Thomasville, North Carolina, to Danville, Virginia. I do not know how she managed to make it with two children in tow, but I do know she somehow succeeded in traversing the seventy-five miles. My mother's courageous decision and action was the turning point in our story.

Howard Myers Jr. (age one)
and brother, Fred Myers (age three)

Once in Danville, my mother was happily reunited with her mother, Bub, and her grandmother, Grandma Berry. Her father, James Parker, liked drinking more than he liked working. He was around only occasionally, as he traveled between Thomasville, North Carolina, and Danville, Virginia, looking for work. To help support our family, my mother went to work in the Danville Cotton Mill.

My mother's courage—to leave behind the darkness of her life with my father's parents to walk into the light of a new life—planted the seeds of resiliency in me. Her love and determination to provide a better life for us left a powerful echo in our lives.

My mom's parents adored their grandchildren, especially me. They worshipped the ground I walked on, so to speak, but wanted me to stay a child. I was terribly spoiled. Grandma Berry, my mother's grandmother, was a kind, high-spirited and loving woman. Grandma Bub did not have a job outside the home, so she was with us most all of the time. She would take me to Fuzzy's Bar to buy me a Coca-Cola and herself a Budweiser, swearing me to secrecy about her love of a cold beer.

One time, Grandma Bub and Grandma Berry were walking with Fred and me, when we passed the tractor store. Grandma Bub said, "Just a minute, I have to pee." She ran to one of the tractor tires, squatted, and relieved herself in front of us. This became quite the comical memory for Fred and me, and a reminder of how times were different back then. On a personal level, I certainly could tell the difference in our new home, these relatives vs. my dad's parents, and my mother's improved disposition as she finally began to feel safe, respected and loved.

While working at the cotton mill, my mother met a man named Jack Pearly Echols. He pushed a lunch wagon and one day my mother walked up to him and asked, "Do you have any good candy?"

Flirting, he responded, "I thought all candy was good."

"But I like Heath bars," she said.

The next day the smitten lunch-wagon pusher came prepared, and when she approached his wagon, he presented her with a Heath bar and a wink.

"What are you trying to do? Make me too big to get through the door?"

"They have bigger doors downstairs," he reassured her.

Jack clocked out at 10:00 p.m. but mom didn't clock out until midnight. He waited for her so they could walk and talk.

"What are you going to do tomorrow?" Jack asked.

Their first date was 2:30 in the afternoon. My mother marveled at the fast-talking auctioneers at the local auctions, so Jack would take her to watch them sell tobacco. They began seeing each other every day from that day forward. Jack would wait for my mother to get off her night shift and have two ham sandwiches and two cups of coffee for them to enjoy as a midnight snack.

One day, my mother and Jack were standing up for her sister Thelma in her wedding, as the maid of honor and best man. Since they were already dressed up and a judge was right there, they decided to get married too! So, only three months after meeting each other, my mother and Jack secretly married. Initially, they stayed in separate homes, my mother at her home and Jack with his parents—but after two weeks they spilled the beans. Nineteen-year-old Jack moved in with his 18-year-old bride, her sons, her mother, and grandmother. Mom's family really liked Jack; he was pleasant, a good worker, and provided money for the household.

From December to May, we lived at my grandmother's. Then, for $250, Jack bought our first house, located in the same town on a small lot next to his brother, Glen. This move was helpful for my mother because she occasionally felt Grandma Bub was interfering with their parenting and privacy. The young couple enjoyed living in their own home, raising us, but that period lasted only four or five years. A friend of Jack's had told him that General Motors was hiring, so they decided to move our young family to Michigan. Jack went north first on a whim! He traveled to Michigan and landed a job at General Motors in Flint, Michigan, in 1953.

My mother's strength and good intuition drove her to make life-changing decisions for my brother and me. In today's world, especially in the United States, I observe how the lack of parenting and leadership in the home is crumbling our nation's values. Parents do the best they can, based on what they know. Fortunately for me, my parents instilled some important values that would help forge my independence.

During the 1940's and 1950's, a strong work ethic and critical life skills were taught in many homes. From a very early age I was taught the importance of work, independence, grit, determination, persistence, and self-reliance. I have had many conversations with my children, friends, and business colleagues about the importance of teaching skills and values to children. I know first-hand that character traits which are developed early in life can impact decisions and actions throughout all the following decades.

My stepfather, Jack Echols, was taught the importance of hard work from a very early age. At the age of four in 1922, he was sent on errands for the family as his older brothers were in school. For example, once little Jack skipped his way to the general store with a dollar in his pocket, well over a mile journey, to purchase a wash tub for the family and get a Coke for five cents. He tucked the bottle into the top of his britches, lifted the wash tub up over his head and marched home with pride.

From a very early age I was taught that chores were a family affair. Everyone in the family did their fair share of work around the house and yard. My new father was a great role model for a strong work ethic. He was a wonderful financial provider for our family. Even today, at age 90, he cultivates his own garden, planting each seed individually and meticulously. He weeds the garden and harvests it, and together with my mother, cans countless batches of wonderful home-grown vegetables. And their yard looks like a picture from Better Homes & Gardens—my father mows it and grooms it with great passion. Without the approval of his children, he even tackles shoveling and snow-blowing the driveway during the harsh Michigan winters.

From the agricultural tobacco mills in the far south to the industrialized factories in the north, my parents have weathered every storm and have stayed committed to their marriage vows. As I am writing this chapter, my parents have been married for 70 years.

Without the life skills my parents instilled in me and without their teaching me the value of work, I would have struggled and failed more in my adult life. They did not just burden my brother and I with chores, they took time to teach us how to do so many practical things, and how to do them correctly. For example, I was taught how to clean a kitchen from top to bottom. My parents would give specific instructions about what needed to be cleaned and what "cleaned" looked like. One Saturday morning my parents left for a few errands and I had an idea I was sure would impress them. I whisked the broom in every corner of the kitchen, filled a pail with water and soap, got down on my hands and knees and scrubbed every inch of the floor, then proceeded to wax the floor. I then moved on, wiped clean the stove, polished it with wax, and proceeded to the refrigerator and polished it to a shine. I washed all the breakfast dishes and marched outside to pick my mother flowers. I dashed back into the house, careful to remove any debris from my bare feet, grabbed a vase and proudly plopped the flowers inside.

Like a private eye, I sat inside and peeked out the window, watching eagerly for their return. Finally, after what seemed like hours, they pulled into the driveway and I opened the door with a big grin on my face. "What kind of trouble did you get yourself into, Howard?" my mother asked. I clutched her hand and guided her to the kitchen to show off my hard work. She praised me for my efforts. My father patrolled the kitchen like an inspector looking at every detail. He was a precise man. Although I had done well as a young boy, my father did find and point out a few flaws that could use improving. That day, my own sense of accomplishment and my mother's approving remarks won out over my disappointment that he was not as pleased as I had hoped. I gradually came to despise the perfection he demanded. It was the same perfection that was demanded of him while growing up, and I now realize that my father was doing his best with what he knew.

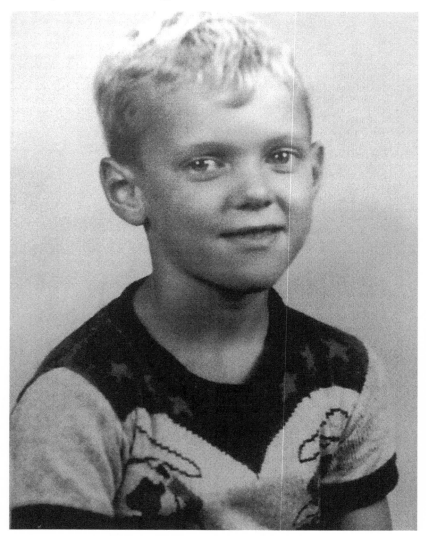

Young Howard Myers, Jr.

Chapter 2: Trauma Begets Trauma, Hope Begets Hope

In addition to hard work, I learned about accountability. I would say that accountability has always been a friend to me throughout my life, starting in my home. It laid the foundation for my journey into my teenage years, giving me the self-confidence and self-reliance that allowed me the freedom of independence at a very early age.

I was not an easy child by any stretch of the imagination. I was a child who liked to test all the boundaries and wore down parents and siblings with my persistence. I began to use my curly blonde hair and deep blue eyes to my advantage and I developed an ability to persuade others that I could do anything I set my mind on. Eventually I became convinced I could charm my way through life. Regardless of my so called self-confidence and independence, I still had a great deal of maturing to do, but my attitude about life was to work hard, play hard.

At the age of 12, I peddled my Schwinn bike five miles to Bauman Farm to learn to milk cows and clean cattle stalls. We bailed hay during the long summer months in mid-Michigan and I still had chores at home to complete regardless of how weary I may have been. Over time, the habits of self-discipline and hard work became second nature to me. I enjoyed the benefits of earning my own money and spending it as I wished. Before long I found myself desiring even more freedom and time. I had the wild idea to trade my daily long bike rides for the luxury of driving the family car along the M-24 highway to the dirt roads of the farm I worked on.

One morning during breakfast I laid out my carefully constructed plan. Like a lawyer, I took control of the room, pleaded my case, and before long I convinced my reluctant judges—my mother and father—to allow me to use their car so I could milk cows before school, drive back home, shower and dress for school, and catch the bus.

Being a farm boy, I was developing a strong, muscular build. Soon I became aware that not only did I enjoy sports, I was strong, fast, and agile. In spite of my already busy schedule, I went out for the track and football teams. Soon it was evident that I was a valuable member of my sport teams. My routine during my teen years, before I bought my first car, consisted of waking at 4:30 in the morning, driving my father's car to milk 40 cows and clean cattle stalls, driving back home to clean up, eat breakfast, and catch the bus to school. I would attend classes, then go to athletic practice, hitch a ride or walk or even jog to the farm 6 miles from school, milk 40 cows and clean the stalls again, walk home, do homework and chores and finally collapse in bed. The next day, I did it all over again.

My family traveled back and forth from Michigan to Danville, Virginia, to stay connected to our roots and family. We learned that my deceased father's parents wanted to see Fred and me. One summer they drove up to Michigan to pick Fred and me up for summer vacation. Fred was asked to come back to the south; I was given a box of socks. My grandmother worked in a sock factory and they felt that the "gift" of socks would ease my pain of being left behind. Man, did that hurt. My new father Jack witnessed this painful encounter and pulled off his wristwatch and gave it to me. His kind and generous act was comforting, but I, like any child, was hurt that I was being excluded. I later was told that they had a special fondness for my brother because he reminded them so much of my father, Howard, who they had lost as a teenager. It's true that Fred looked very much like him.

At times life may not seem fair, or we wonder why certain events do not seem to go our way, yet years later I can see how not visiting my deceased father's parents may have protected my young mind from negativity. Over the years, my brother's visits with his pessimistic grandparents would not only affect his mindset but would profoundly influence my adolescent mind and programming.

"In fairytales, he is the brave, noble, chivalrous man who comes to the rescue of the fair, helpless damsel in distress, asking nothing in return for his good deeds.
In the real world, well, things are a bit more complicated."

—*Eduard Ezeanu*

Chapter 3
The Gallant Knight

Have you ever wondered how in the world you ever survived your childhood and teen years? My childhood was often a far cry from positivity for me. In fact, you might say that young Howard Myers was programmed and influenced in a number of deleterious ways. As a young teenager in the late 1950's, I was exposed to some destructive practices that had a powerful influence on my life. I'm reminded of what early computer programmers described as: Garbage in=Garbage out.

Around the age of 13, I sometimes was sent to visit my extended family in Virginia and North Carolina. I loved seeing my aunts, uncles, and cousins, and I always looked forward to those times. However, these visits influenced me, as I see it now, with a lot of "garbage in." Prejudice, misogyny, violence, and criminal behavior were just some of the dark seeds planted in my impressionable young mind.

One of my relatives was a leader in the Ku Klux Klan. One night we were out partying, drinking beer and raising hell, like normal, and my uncle said to me, "Watch this boy dance, Howard." Then he pulled out a pistol and started shooting toward the ground, laughing while a black man ran away from us down the street. Another time, a black man pulled into my uncle's gas station.

The man wanted to buy a dollar's worth of gasoline. I watched in stunned silence as my uncle pulled out a pistol, put it to the driver's head, and said, "If I ever see you at this gas station again, I will blow your brains out." Yes, I often witnessed this type of appalling behavior; in their world, it was considered a norm.

Besides the blatant racism, I was also exposed to some pretty sketchy criminal activity. My relatives allowed my brother and me to drink alcohol in the backseat of their car while they drove around on "errands." What they were doing, in actuality, was transporting moonshine. One night, my uncle looked back to us in the rear seat and said, "Watch this, boys!" The car accelerated and we sped off down the road, the lights of some federal agents following us. We flew along until another one of my relatives used his car to block the Feds, letting us get away. I remember looking out the car's back window, thinking…*this is so cool!* Clearly, my moral development was being shaped in very wrong-minded ways.

Another time, my brother and I went to an after-hours club with our aunts and uncles who permitted us to drink booze. I was around 13 at the time and was dancing with one of my uncles when a man walked up and said, "Two guys can't dance together." My uncle grabbed him by the throat and growled, "Who is gonna stop us, boy? The hell you gonna do about it?" My uncle threw the guy away from him. I watched in amazement as the man got up off the floor and just walked away.

Then there was the misogyny, which manifested itself as womanizing. I didn't understand what I was seeing at the time, but later I realized how poorly some of my Virginia and North Carolina relatives treated the women in their lives. They ran around on their wives, doing things they really should not have been doing. As impressionable as I was at that time, I thought their behavior was normal—even admirable—and I did my best to emulate it.

I'm happy to report that my uncles' lives (and my own!) changed drastically over the years—for the better. They traded carousing, chaos, and drama for sanity, simplicity, and honesty. They started going to church, and they acted like married men and good citizens instead of self-centered hoodlums.

It wasn't until many years after I grew up that I began to comprehend how the attitudes I had learned and behaviors I practiced were hurting me instead of helping me. I'm not really proud of many of the things that I did while growing up. I was one crazy young man whose actions were profoundly influenced by the negativity I'd seen as a youngster. I did not know how to be authentic and genuine or how to be supportive of the opposite sex. There were so many heartaches I suffered, and caused for others, because of so much "garbage in."

***

As in anything, not everything in my upbringing was negative. There had to have been positive influences as well, for when I reflect back on my life I recall myself as an independent young man who believed that he could be, do, or have anything he wanted—with the right belief, effort, and the right attitude.

As a result, I was able to achieve some incredible things. Because I believed that I could run faster than anyone else, for several years I held several high school track records. I served as a captain on the football team and, because I believed that I could score more touchdowns than anyone else, I once scored four touchdowns playing as a running back in a high school football game.

At the young age of fifteen, because I believed in myself and understood the value of hard work, I was able to convince my mother and father that I needed to move out and work on a farm. So I moved out of my home and onto the Kelly farm, where I was given room and board and was paid $20 a week to milk cows every morning before school and again each evening.

I kept going to school and playing sports. I wouldn't say I did very well academically because I never was interested in school—just sports and girls. While I loved being independent, it wasn't cheap, so I took another job. On the weekends, I worked at the Standard Gas filling station.

When I turned 16, Walt Kelly, my boss at the farm, helped me buy my first car. It was a 1957 Chevrolet. I remember vividly my overwhelming excitement. I took great pride in keeping my Chevy shined and polished—it might not have been the best-looking car in the neighborhood, but it definitely was the cleanest and shiniest.

I worked on the Kelly farm and at the Standard Gas station from ages 15 to 18, until I graduated from high school in 1964. During those years, I also moonlighted at a few small machine shops—any way to make some money to go out and have fun. It didn't take much in those days to fill up my car with gas and take my girlfriend out to dinner and a movie. I could have as much fun as I needed with $10, and I always had money left over at the end of the week. That's how we lived in the '60s.

***

After I graduated from high school, I thought I was going to be a gallant knight and take my high school sweetheart Kristi away from her miserable home and dysfunctional family. We decided we were going to run away and get married. At the time, it sounded like a logical plan to two teenage kids.

Howard, age 17

She was 17, and I was 19. I had a 1964 Plymouth Fury, a brand new car that I had bought off the show room floor after I had gone to work for Buick Motors. I thought I was filthy rich, making $150 a week and working as much overtime as I could get. Back then, that really was good money.

I had picked Kristi up from school one morning, and all she could talk about was how terrible her life was. So we decided to run away and get married right then, just out of the blue. We took off with a couple hundred dollars in my pocket in my new

Fury, four-on-the-floor. Another couple, Danny Kelch and Karen Gallagher, decided to go along with us to get married as well, since Karen had recently found out that she was expecting.

The four of us zoomed off into our wild blue yonder. I remember turning up the song on the radio. It was "Catch Us If You Can," by the Dave Clark Five, and we were going across the Michigan-Ohio border, laughing and carrying on as young people do, thinking we had the world by the ass and we had all the answers.

We drove down to Virginia to my uncle's place and hid my car since we thought maybe somebody, the law, might be looking for us. We borrowed my Uncle Doug's car and drove to South Carolina to get married. I was the only one old enough to get married legally, so everybody else had changed their birth certificates. The Justice of the Peace put them under a light and said, "These birth certificates have been changed. You kids get out of here. I'm not marrying you."

We proceeded to have a honeymoon without a marriage. Danny's mother and Karen's mother found out where we were and drove down to get them. Kristi and I stayed a little bit longer, and then we drove back home to face the music.

If I thought it was bad when we left, it was holy hell when we got back. Kristi's parents would not let us see each other. But forbidding something is stupid, because teenagers see it as a challenge. We snuck around and got together every time we could. One Saturday night, I went over to pick up Kris. I waited for her folks to go out to dinner as they always did on Saturday evenings. I was waiting down the road at Barnes Lake, watching for them to leave so I could sneak up to the house and get Kristi. But that night, Kristi's stepdad saw my car sitting there, and I said, *Well, I might as well own up to the truth*, whatever that might have meant at that time. I drove down to their house and got out of the car.

Paul, Kristi's stepdad, walked out into the road to ask me what I was doing. We got into a confrontation and argument. Virginia, Kristi's mom, came out and said a few choice words to me, and I shot a few choice words back.

"What did you call my wife?" Paul asked.

"I didn't say any more to her than she did to me," I retorted.

The next thing I knew, a big fist hit me in the face. He didn't knock me down, just back. I shook my head and came running toward him, figuring I'd head-butt and tackle him and kick his ass. I managed to head-butt him and knocked him down on the road. We were out in the road fighting. Kristi was yelling at her mother. Then she and I jumped in the car and spun out to get away.

There was no reasoning with us. Finally, Kristi's mother agreed to sign for her to get married, and we got married on February 11, 1966. We got married at the Pilgrim Holiness Church in North Branch, Michigan. My parents attended, as did Kristi's. Then we took off afterwards to Niagara Falls.

In hindsight, it's easy for me to say that I should never have gotten married at that age. I did not have a clue about what I was doing. Kristi and I were very immature and had no real understanding of what marriage and commitment meant or what a healthy relationship required. We both had experienced a lot of dysfunction in our younger years, and we did the best that we could.

After Kristi and I got married, I continued to work at Buick until one day I decided that I wasn't going to be told what to do. I grew up on a farm knowing how to work, and the foremen really took advantage of the farm boys that came to work at the factory. I think that I knew deep down that working for GM for three decades was not for me. I had a passion for life! I wanted more than the hamster wheel daily grind: get up, go to work, go home, try to be a good husband, watch TV, go to bed, and do it all over again, day after day. I was tired of being a spectator and watching my life go by.

I remember the day I quit my job. I had been working there for almost two years. That day, the foreman came down and said, "Hey, Myers. Can you catch a job for the new hire who works down the line from you?"

"I'll help when I can," I said.

Sometime later, he came down the floor and got in my face. "I thought I told you to catch that job!"

"No," I said, "you asked me."

"No, I'm telling you!"

I told him to kiss my ass, and I was out of there. I punched out on the time clock, went home, didn't have a job, and didn't have a clue to what I was doing. It was summertime and I spent the evening wondering how I was going to provide for myself and my new wife.

That's when I decided that I was going to sign up for the draft. Maybe going into the military would teach me how to grow up and be responsible and more mature. A lot of my friends were being drafted at that time, but I had a deferment because of my left hand. I had injured it as a child when I fell on a piece of sharp glass and permanently severed a tendon. So, soon after I left the Buick plant, I went down to the draft board to convince the lady down there that there wasn't really anything wrong with my hand.

"I can go in the service," I told her. "This hand is fine."

She agreed, and I signed up. (It was during the Viet Nam War and recruitment was in full force.)

The dirty little secret was that I never told my wife, Kristi, that I was signing up for the draft. Instead, I told her I was drafted. Maybe unconsciously I was running away from my marriage. Maybe I was running away from myself.

"It is forbidden to kill; therefore all murderers are punished…
unless they kill in large numbers and to the sound of trumpets."

—Voltaire

Chapter 4
Tigerland

Ready to exchange my boyhood immaturity for becoming a man,
I boarded the bus in Lapeer, Michigan, headed to Detroit, where
I got a physical. Then I caught a train to Fort Knox, Kentucky,
for U.S. Army boot camp.

Howard, third row, 6ᵗʰ from right; US Army boot camp,
Fort Knox, Kentucky (1966)

The military was a real challenge for me because I approached it as a competition to be the best that I could be. I prided myself on being one of the fastest, strongest men in my company. This North Branch Michigan football and track star ranked tops in basic training. It should have occurred to me that as one of the best of my company of 300, I was much more likely to be sent to Fort Polk, Louisiana, to be trained to fight in Vietnam. It should have been no surprise when I was selected as one of those first from my company to go to Tigerland.

This military training base was set up to give us advanced, individual training. Part of Fort Polk was filled with dense jungle-like vegetation, making it ideal for preparing soldiers for conditions like those in Vietnam.

I remember arriving in Fort Polk, Louisiana—also known among troops as Fort Puke, LousyAnna. It was hot and humid and downright miserable. Being one of the first into the barracks, I crawled up into my bunk and pulled the pillow over my head, crying. *What in the world is happening to my life? What am I doing here? Am I really going to Vietnam?* This was my reward for being a so-called man. I was a fast, competitive, and strong specimen…I was also just a scared little boy.

Each morning I awoke to the sound of the trumpet playing reveille.

> *You've got to get up*
> *You've got to get up*
> *You've got to get up this morning*
> *You've got to get up*
> *You've got to get up*
> *Get up with the bugler's call.*
> *The major told the captain*
> *The captain told the sergeant*
> *The sergeant told the bugler*
> *The bugler told them all.*

Howard arrives at Tigerland, Fort Polk, Louisiana (1967)

Training at Tigerland started at 5 o'clock every morning and ended at 11 p.m. each night. This training was more intense than anything I'd experienced in boot camp. We ran more, drilled more, and slept less. Every day we ran before breakfast, after breakfast, and after drills.

Basically, it seemed we were running all day long. We kept running and running, just like Forrest Gump.

Training also took place in classrooms: it was very difficult to stay awake to learn how to keep yourself alive, in a war, in a foreign country. We were in classes each day, learning about weapons. I was trained to use three major weapons: a 106mm anti-tank recoilless gun mounted on a jeep or armored personnel carrier, a 50 caliber machine gun, and an M16 rifle. We were training all day in something. There were no breaks.

Howard, a Tigerland warrior

I was being brainwashed to do the extraordinary. Army training prepared me mentally and physically but the emotional piece became a blur... *Was I going to die, or was I going to kill someone?* I became friends with self-discipline; I trained like a man. It became obvious that, being young and having fertile minds, we young men were the perfect specimens.

Each barrack had to be cleaned each evening with the floors spotless, foot lockers organized, and boots shining. Each one of us had to obey these orders. If anyone failed to shine their shoes or have their locker organized, the entire platoon could not go to sleep. If we were caught falling asleep in classes or anywhere on the grounds we were punished. I could never recall being so exhausted and sleep-deprived.

One particular day my exhaustion overcame me. I started nodding off to sleep, my head bobbing up and down, eyes snapping shut. I mustered every ounce of strength to fight off sleep but it was useless. We were sitting on the bleachers receiving a lecture. My sergeant got in my face and screamed, "Myers, you just volunteered for cattle guard around the compound tonight instead of sleeping!" Cattle guard was a harassment technique used to punish us if we disobeyed any orders, including falling asleep. For several hours I walked around with my M16 rifle searching for wild boar in the pitch dark. I was checked on multiple times by the sergeant until finally I was ordered to go to bed. I crawled and collapsed into my bunk, drifted off to sleep only to be rudely wakened by our sergeant at 5 a.m. yelling and barking orders. "Get out of bed, assholes!" "Rise and shine, ladies!" I was frightened out of a deep sleep and sat up like a jack-in-the-box, jumped to the floor and began to dress in my fatigues and lace up my boots. I seriously wondered how I was going to make it another day. I was miserable, scared, exhausted. I wanted out!

For the first four weeks we had no privileges at all. If we obeyed all orders we were given permission to call home to talk a short time to family. I remember standing in long lines to use the pay phone. I dialed my first wife Kristi and pleaded for her help, begging for her to find a way to get me out of Tigerland. I told her to contact the Red Cross and tell them "I was losing my mind" and I needed help. On the other end of the phone my wife said, "There is nothing I can do, Howard!" My futile attempt only caused me to sink deeper into fear and miss my former life back home. My wife assured me that I could make it a few more weeks, then she would arrive for a long weekend visit when I earned my weekend pass.

The next day, we were ordered to hike 20 miles with full backpacks, ammunition, and our M16 rifles in the hot, steamy, heavy air, up and down hills. We were told if we dropped out and quit on this hike, we would not be allowed any weekend passes. After our all-day hike there were only a few of us boys left standing and I was one of them. My goal to see my wife was enough to keep me from quitting. My self-discipline became my friend this day and I was developing perseverance and grit. I trained my mind to go one step at a time. My feet throbbing with pain, my back pack weighing down on my thinning frame, my clothes soaking wet, I marched forward with the end in mind, knowing I would be reunited for a short time with my wife.

Finally the weekend arrived and I was granted my weekend pass. Kristi took a flight to Shreveport, Louisiana. I was determined to find a way to see my young wife. I had to hitchhike over 100 miles to meet up with her from Fort Polk. I packed my weekend bag, threw it over my shoulder and strutted out of Tigerland to find a series of rides. I found my way to the main highway and stuck up my thumb hoping someone would soon stop and give me a ride. Dressed in military khakis with my duffle bag, it did not take long before a trucker stopped and asked me where I was headed. "Shreveport, Louisiana," I said, "to meet my bride for one weekend."

I saw some compassion in his eyes as he looked down at me. "Hop in, soldier!" He took me all the way to my destination. Once my wife and I were reunited, we held one another for hours. We laughed, cried, and shared stories. I heard what was taking place back home, and I shared what boot camp and Tigerland was like. We were on a roller coaster ride of emotions and the weekend slipped away like a dream.

When it was time for our departure, the pain and emptiness of my "reality" sat back in. I stood next to my young wife and watched her pack her personal belongings into her suitcase. I admired her courage, her beauty, and I truly felt in love. We took a taxi to the airport. I remember walking her to the terminal and holding her in my arms, both of us crying and longing for more time together. It was one of the most difficult moments in my young life, watching her walk away to the plane. We both were experiencing the reality of war! I was heading back into my reality and she was traveling back to hers. I stood there transfixed, nearly in shock knowing I had to let her go…and that I had to hitchhike to get back to Fort Polk before 9 p.m.

Kristi Myers, Shreveport, Louisiana, (1967)

After experiencing my emotional weekend with my wife, I began to dream of her more and more, wondering what she was doing back home. One particular day I was training to set up a claymore mine and my mind began to wander back home. I was obviously not focused on my task because I was setting up my claymore mine backwards. One of my sergeants, who had just returned from Nam, was carrying a big stick and struck it against my helmet, ringing my bell, screaming, "You are an asshole, soldier! You are one of those idiots who are going to go over to Nam and get your ass blown up!" Little did I know the truth in his statement.

I often wonder if I was destined for more trauma. Only a few months earlier I was in basic training and I had just dug up a mock landmine. I began to disarm it—by touch, not by sight—but once again my mind was back home and not in the present moment. I looked down to see what I had done wrong when a firecracker-type device exploded in my face and blackened my eyes with soot. This event embarrassed me, but now I look back and realize this may have been destiny. As I often admit, becoming blind has never been easy but it may have saved my life.

Tigerland was more than just physical training. We were also being programmed to have the mindset of a killer. There were eerie reminders placed throughout Fort Polk; some call it propaganda, brainwashing or programming, while others call it preparing for war. Signs were peppered throughout our training facility: TIGERLAND VILLAGE, VILLAGE WARFARE WITH THE ENEMY VIET CONG, FIGHT WIN! One large wooden sign displayed the image of an oriental man hiding in the rice paddies with the words, THE ENEMY. VIET CONG. Another: AGGRESSIVENESS AND FIRE POWER WILL WIN! My mind was slowly changing with the drip, drip, drip of reminders that I was no longer allowed to be a boy but faced a duty that I was not yet emotionally prepared for.

Tigerland soldiers also had to growl every time we went outside. We had to growl every time we did pushups. We had to growl every time a command was given to us. And we had to, of course, always do WHATEVER they told us to do. At the time, I was not aware of how my mind was reshaping. Now, in my 70s, I look back and remember my platoon marching in cadence on the way to church chanting, "I want to go to Vietnam! I want to kill a Vietcong! Kill! Kill! Kill!" My fertile young mind was being cultivated as a killing machine.

A lot of fights went on in those nine weeks of training. Of course, I happened to be in one of them. A small-framed black guy bunked beneath me. Every morning, as I was lacing up my boots, he managed to brush up against me with his ass, pretending he needed to get past me. One thing led to another and a fight started. It was the '60s. All the whites got on one side, and all the blacks got on the other. I don't believe anyone got hurt very badly that day, but it was a sign of the tension and sleep-deprivation we were all feeling. Not to mention the testosterone overload! You train young men to be killers, and they're going to look for a fight.

Nine weeks after that little boy crawled into his bunk and cried about his future, he was a killer who walked boldly up to the Captain. I shook his hand and thanked him for teaching me how to be a man and told him that I was "ready to go to 'Nam and kill some VC!"

I went from Fort Polk, Louisiana, to Fort Dix, New Jersey. That's where they were shipping us out to go to Vietnam. The weekend before we were to be shipped, Ron Minton, one of my best friends at that time, and I snuck off on a Friday morning and went AWOL. We cajoled some pals to call out our service numbers when roster was called over the weekend. I had no idea what the consequences were, I just followed my heart and intuition and took the risk. *What are they gonna do? Send me to Vietnam?*

Ron and I hitchhiked to the airport, got a flight back to Detroit and spent the weekend home with our families. I wanted to spend as much time as possible with my wife, and take my Plymouth Fury out for a spin. We were out on the back roads late into the evening. The rain came and the dirt roads changed into mud. After what seemed like hours, I gave up on my futile attempts to get my car unstuck. I placed my wife on my back and hauled ass out of the mud. I began pounding on the doors of nearby homes, pleading with strangers to use a phone to call my stepfather. Finally, after several attempts, one kind stranger let me use the phone. We made it out just in time for my flight, so I was back to Fort Dix by Monday morning when they called roster and prepared to send us out on a TWA flight. (As it turned out, this was the weekend my son Chad was conceived.)

I remember the flight over to Vietnam. It seemed to take forever to get there. It was a commercial TWA flight full of a bunch of soldiers. The in-flight movie was a bit ironic: *Born Free.* We made a stop in Hawaii and had to walk through the terminals to get to our next transport. I tried to order a beer, but was refused. *Old enough to go to Vietnam, not old enough to buy a beer.* For some reason, there were several movie stars in the airport that day. In particular, I recall seeing Ursula Andress, a sexy blonde actress. Man! White pants, a halter top and no bra. She is one of my last visual memories of the States…a beautiful one at that.

> "All the art of living lies in a fine mingling of
> letting go and holding on."
>
> —*Havelock Ellis*

Chapter 5
My New Reality

BOOM! The lights went out. My life, as I knew it, was over.

I was conscious but in shock, so my memories of the explosion and its aftermath are scattered and dreamlike. I remember hearing the whump, whump, whump of the helicopter flying in to transport us to a field hospital. Wounded soldiers were moaning for help.

"Look at me first!" one young man cried. "I am worse off than that guy!"

Someone else called, "Oh God, help me!"

Hands lifted me off the armored personnel carrier and placed me on a stretcher. I felt very cold, which was strange because it was monsoon season: 100 degrees and 100 percent humidity. I moaned and screamed in fear. The pain was too much to bear. I felt myself slip in and out of consciousness. I was in shock! I wanted to open my eyes to see the aftermath of the landmine explosion but I could not see my reality. The medics kept trying to keep me from losing consciousness as they transported me to a field hospital. Every cell in my body wanted to lose consciousness to escape the pain. Little did I know my reality would never be the same.

After we arrived at the field hospital, I was wheeled into an operating room. Slipping in and out of consciousness, I was aware that I was only wearing my fatigues and combat boots. Despite the pain and confusion, my mind reminded me I'd been lying in a rice paddy the night before, and when I got back to our camp, I had exchanged my soaking wet fatigues for some dry ones. I decided not to put on any underwear because mine were in such bad shape I figured they would rot before I had a chance to get a shower. "Nurse, nurse!" I said with some urgency, "I don't have any underwear on!"

She replied, "Hey soldier, this is not my first rodeo." And then someone started cutting off my fatigues, a needle slipped into my arm, and I went under…

I don't know if it was a few hours or a few days later, but I awoke in a field hospital crying out for help. The pain in my head and legs was horrid. A band had been brought in for the soldiers' entertainment. My window was open, and I could hear tambourines and maracas. The noise caused me so much agony, I screamed, "Shut the hell up!" My head hurt so bad, I couldn't stand it. The pain, as I would later learn, was caused by many factors. I was scared. I reached up to feel my face and discovered thick gauze patches covering both of my eyes.

One of the causes of the intense pain I was suffering was the injury to my nose. When they fixed my nose—it had been blown loose—they had to pack the wound with 36 inches of gauze. When it was finally removed, I felt immediate relief from some of the pressure in my head.

Maybe they told me what had happened and I was just too drugged up to remember it. Or maybe they didn't want to give me the bad news until I was back in the States. In any case, I didn't learn until much later that my nose had been blown loose and the doctors had sewn it back on. I also had holes in my leg and arm from shrapnel.

At the time, however, because my eyes were covered, I could not see myself to judge my condition. In a state of utter panic, I started screaming at the top of my lungs for someone to tell me what had happened. I wanted some answers! I had no idea what they had done or how much time had passed since the explosion. Some celebrity guy touring for the soldiers came by and tried to talk with me. Out of my mind with pain and anxiety, I ignored his kindness and said, "I don't give a shit who you are! I need someone who can give me some answers!" I found out later that he was Brian Kelly, then the star of the hit television show "Flipper." I have to assume that if he was caring enough to come to visit wounded soldiers, he was generous enough to have forgiven me.

I was moved from field hospital to field hospital before I was transferred back to the States, and I still did not know the extent of my injuries. Finally, I was admitted to a hospital in Valley Forge, Pennsylvania, where I spent nearly five weeks. While I was at the hospital in Valley Forge, I turned 21. My nurse must have felt some sympathy for me because she brought me a beer to help me celebrate. Unfortunately, I got extremely ill because of all the medicine I was taking for pain.

My wife Kristi came and stayed with me for a few weeks to help me through my fear. I was afraid to go to the bathroom. I was afraid to walk anywhere. I was afraid of everything. What made matters worse was the constant moaning I heard from a three-star general; his cry, "I am dying, I am dying!" echoed through our hallways, haunting me.

My terrified little child was back. Despite all the meds pumped into me to eliminate my suffering, the only thing that really relieved my pain and fear was my expectant wife sitting next to me, holding my hand, supporting me emotionally. I was beginning to learn the touch of another caring human being was very important to my healing, as it is for all of us. Kristi assured me, despite her own fears and anxiety, that with God's help we would make it. In retrospect, I never could have made it through those early days without the support and strength of that warrior woman. She knew she had to be responsible and strong for our expected child and for me. I was a scared soldier boy, not having a clue about what the future might bring. I wondered what kind of a father and husband was I going to be. I drew enough strength from Kristi to somehow make it through, one day at a time, until I was told I would be leaving Valley Forge.

*Lucy Echols (Howard's mother), Howard, and Kristi
(VA hospital, Valley Forge, Pennsylvania)*

*Howard's stepfather, Jack, on left; other family and close
friends visiting VA hospital, Valley Forge, Pennsylvania*

I was then transferred to Fort Dix, New Jersey (for one day), on my way to my final destination: the Central Blind Rehabilitation Center, Edward Hines, Jr. VA Hospital in Chicago, Illinois. When I walked into the Center, usually referred to as "Hines," I still had patches over both of my eyes. I figured I was there so the eye patches could finally be removed and they could check on the progress of my many weeks of healing. I was excited to finally be able to see the light of day, though I anticipated it would be a harsh adjustment at first.

Hines VA Blind Rehabilitation Center(Chicago, Illinois)

Once I was settled in my room, I was told they would be making prosthetic eyes for me. "What are you talking about?" I asked. It was only then—six weeks after the explosion—that I was told I had no eyes. I finally knew why my head had felt so acutely painful: they had removed my eyes and given me replacement implants.

Throughout the entire experience after the explosion, the communication I received about the extent of my injuries and the actions the doctors and army were taking regarding my care was shockingly vague and incomplete.

I don't remember much from Valley Forge, only what I was *not* told. When you're not told anything, and you are stuck in the dark both figuratively and literally, it is easy to imagine *anything*. My mind started delving into dark prospects.

It's difficult to explain how frustrated and impotent I felt when no one would answer my questions. I'd no idea that I was going to be blind for the rest of my life. The only clue was when a social worker came in and handed me a stylus and slate, telling me that I would probably need to learn how to use these items. I knew that those were tools that blind people used, but that was the extent of the communication. So I spent a lot of that time contemplating the unknown. The uncertainty was maddening. I didn't realize at that time that God was going to be the how and the rest was up to me.

So that day at the hospital in Chicago I finally got my answer. It was shocking, to say the least. I was going to be totally blind for the rest of my life.

At first, I was filled with intense anger, followed by fear and severe depression. I had no desire to face the reality of living the rest of my life without the capacity for sight. *What the hell kind of life would that be?*

When I showed up at the Hines Rehab Center, I was too afraid to even get out of bed to go to the bathroom by myself. Underlying my fear was a well of embarrassment and deep-rooted shame. Because I had been such an independent man from a young age, and a football and track star in high school, I could not help wondering what I was going to do with my life. I could envision myself sitting on a corner selling pencils. I was somehow ashamed of my injuries. When I had to walk somewhere, I would never hang onto anyone. Instead, I walked beside them, trying to pretend that I could see, touching their arm now and again to make sure I was not straying.

I had no idea what I looked like or how the surgeries had changed my appearance. I know now that my nose is wider. I used to have a narrow nose, but the injury and surgery spread it out a bit. I truly was embarrassed because I had no idea how people looked at me, and I had preconceived ideas of what a blind person looked like.

The staff at Hines had to teach me all the basics. I was like a child; I had to learn how to eat, dress, walk, clean, cook, read, and communicate in a new way. It was extremely frightening because I did not know how to do any of this until I was taught. I had to start all over again. I had to move through my fears daily and master the art of resiliency. Through repetition, I had to relearn everything. First, I had to learn how to walk from the bed to the bathroom with a cane. Imagine every night—you can no longer use the night light to find the bathroom. You cannot turn on the light to find the toilet, or the sink. So many things we all take for granted.

I wanted to take pride in my appearance. I wanted to dress well with matching clothes; I did not want to look like a blind guy dressed me. I had to learn how to match my clothes, including my socks. For example, my brown socks were tied and my black socks were folded. I had to create new systems of how to find things with touch. In essence, I was rewiring my brain from sight to touch and sound. Over and over again, I relearned basic skills we all take for granted, like walking.

To ease our pain and forget about our worries we played practical jokes—blind jokes—on one another. We created cheap entertainment to lighten our darkness, dumping salt and pepper all over the food of the other blind residents when they were not looking. Being a new recruit at Hines was not easy. Sometimes we would type letters to folks back home using typewriters. We decided it was humorous to distract the new blind residents so they would lose their place and then type over the text they had already typed.

We were told to hang our canes on the back of our doors. Being foolish and youthful we would twist the canes, bend them to make walking with the cane nearly impossible. We especially picked on the older, grumpy guys. *What were they going to do? Put me in a line up with other blind guys to be identified by a blind guy?*

We had several means of entertainment from blind bingo to blind golf. Hines teamed up with different country clubs and club volunteers offered us a day of golf from time to time, bringing us drinks, dinners, and chasing our balls. Volunteers would guide me in the right direction and describe where the green was located, giving me an approximate distance. When I did reach the green someone would wiggle the pole in the hole, creating a rattling sound so I could hear where to putt. I was able to hit some very decent drives. I would squat down, line my driver up and stand up. The caddie would point me in the right direction and I would take several practice swings. I would again squat down to feel the ball. Over time I was able to hit the ball with incredible accuracy.

I must acknowledge the Center and staff at Hines. The program then (and it continues today for all visually impaired veterans) consisted of classes for us on skill areas including Living Skills, Manual Skills, Orientation, and Mobility. The objective: Independence.

The staff started helping me learn to move from my hospital room to the bathroom. Then they taught me to walk around the hospital. I learned how to find landmarks, first in the hospital, then on the hospital grounds, and then in nearby subdivisions. They taught me how to cross a highway by tuning into sounds. There was always someone close by so I wouldn't get hurt, but they taught me independence and how to live life on my terms.

By the time I left, the Hines staff had started rebuilding my confidence, I began creating road maps in my mind, using my imagination to navigate in a sighted world. I was there a total of 18 weeks. In those four-and-a-half months, I re-learned and re-thought how to read, write, and walk. They gave me the basic tools to survive, to become independent, and to create as much freedom as I wanted to create.

The Hines staff "graduated" me by dropping me off in the middle of a field, where I had to "feel" the sun to find my way back to the hospital. I had to focus my attention on sounds and use my other senses to guide me. Maybe my young fertile mind gave me an advantage of learning quickly and in starting to overcome my challenges. By the time I left Hines, I was able to travel in downtown Chicago with my cane, crossing eight lanes of traffic.

The staff at Hines was wonderful, and I was greatly encouraged by one friend I made there, Milt Jo. He was a fellow patient at the rehab center, a World War II veteran, and we became good friends despite our twenty-year age difference. We would hang out and party and get into trouble together. You will learn more about Milt later. If you ever have an opportunity to give encouragement and inspiration to someone by how you live your life, don't squander that opportunity. Also, if you ever find that someone has come into your life that brings light into your darkest hour, pay attention. They are there for a reason, so don't waste the opportunity to learn from them.

I looked at all my training at Hines like a challenge, and my competitive nature helped push me to do my very best. Once I was informed of my new reality, I knew that this was going to be my world and my life. I began exchanging my anger for hope. I began to let go and accept the responsibility of owning my blindness, knowing this is a process we all have to go through to release the trauma and heal.

I remember my wife coming to pick me up from Hines VA Hospital. She described to me a young blind solider sitting in the wheelchair with patches over his eyes, most likely blind, with no legs, waiting for his turn to learn his new reality. As my young wife wheeled me out of the hospital, it dawned on me that someone, somewhere, was worse off than I was. I reflected on the experience of what happened in Vietnam, and I left Hines feeling less sorry for myself and more hopeful for a brighter future.

Near the end of my stay at Hines, I was presented with the Purple Heart, given to those who are wounded or killed in military battle. I felt both confused and proud. My parents, my wife Kristi, and a few close friends attended the ceremony. Again, my emotions were a blur—the Vietnam War never made any sense to me.

Howard receiving last minute instructions
before Purple Heart ceremony (November, 1967)

Kristi and Howard, Purple Heart Ceremony (November 1967)

"Reject your sense of injury and the injury itself disappears."

— Marcus Aurelius

Chapter 6
The Blind Leading the Blind

I met Milt Jo at Hines VA Hospital at one of the social events we had each Thursday night. He was around 45 at the time, a totally blind WWII veteran. Women from the community would come and spend time with all of us, dance, play games, and socialize. Milt was a ladies' man. Right away I picked up on Milt's charm and listened to how he spoke with confidence to everyone, especially the women. Man, could he flirt!

Milt and I connected almost immediately. And so our friendship began—a young 21-year-old blind Vietnam veteran hanging out with someone old enough to be my father. Milt taught me many things. Perhaps not all of his influence was "good," but having him in my life at that precise time made a profound and lasting impression on me, and I could not have more gratitude.

Milt, despite his circumstances and lack of sight, lived life with gusto. I had no time whatsoever to develop a bitter, woe-is-me attitude with Milt right there beside me.

One evening Milt decided to call a taxi to take us around Chicago to go bar-hopping. Each of us had a cane and we tapped our way into the bars, asked for drinks and socialized. We both drank more than one too many.

When the taxi driver dropped us off back at the VA hospital, we found our way to our rooms, banging our canes and laughing as we passed through the building, careening down the halls, waking up patients. Milt and I decided it would be a good idea to take the jukebox out of the community center and wheel it down to my room, plug it in, and dance. It just so happened that I had a bottle of rum hidden away for special occasions. We sang, danced, and raised hell. The night staff did not know what to do with us.

The next morning the director of the blind rehab center at Hines called Milt and me into his office after hearing from the staff of our adventures. He yelled and screamed and then threatened to kick us out of the program if we did not straighten up. Our response was, "Who cares?!" Once he saw our response and attitude, he told us to go back to class and it was forgotten.

The connection I had with Milt helped create some of the important skills I would need later in life as I was adapting to blindness. His confidence glowed and was contagious. His voice had conviction; I wanted to be more like Milt. In many ways he was like a blind father to me, teaching me the importance of letting go of my blindness as a "problem" and to accept it like a man. Milt was always upbeat and positive and I never, ever saw him feeling sorry for himself. Milt's independence and sense of freedom inspired me, so when we finally graduated from blind rehab, I decided I would fly out to San Francisco alone to meet Milt for a Las Vegas trip.

We flew to Las Vegas together—two blinded veterans, dressed in suits and ready to take on Sin City. Upon arriving at the Flamingo resort, we informed the front desk we were both blind and would need a taxi as well as help around the strip. No problem. We gambled, went to a few shows, drank, and raised some hell. There was nothing Milt and I could not do. I was learning more and more independence and confidence that would help set the stage for greater things in my future.

Not too long after that, Milt decided to come to Michigan to spend some time with my family and me. We sat around and discussed what we used to do when we were younger, before the service, before we lost our eyesight. I told stories about how I had enjoyed water skiing on my in-law's lake, where Kristi, my first wife, had grown up. For some reason, I decided right then to ski again, for the first time blinded. Kristi drove us to her parents' home and started up the speed boat as I prepared by putting on my skis in the dark of my blindness, visualizing the lake.

I gripped the rope handle tightly and said, "Hit it!" I went under, forgetting to lean back and trust the boat to pull me up. We tried again and again until finally, I leaned back and let the boat pull me up—something I had done so easily when sighted. Through repetition, I now knew to just trust the process, the driver, and the boat. Before long, I was skiing in and out of wakes and getting more and more confident, so I decided to drop a ski. I was slalom water skiing! I thought *if I can do this, I can do anything!*

I glided back and forth across the lake that I had once skied on while sighted, but now I was doing this with blind vision. I was grinning and having the time of my life, when suddenly, I heard people screaming, "Dock! Dock! DOCK!" I was confused, frightened, and since I was completely unaware of my surroundings, I dropped the ski rope and went under water. Later, I learned that only a few feet away was a dock, full of people. I bobbed up and down as the bystanders looked on in total disbelief of how close I had come to hitting their dock and sustaining serious injuries. We refined my skiing to make it safer, and I continued to ski for many years, well into my 40's. Water skiing gave me the confidence to try other sports over the years.

Howard in his late 30's—Slalom Water Skiing (Michigan)

"Fit and fun" became a theme for me. I was in the best shape of my life, working out daily, lifting weights, and becoming stronger and stronger. At one stretch of time, in my early twenties to late twenties, I had 19-inch arms and I was bench pressing 350 pounds. Experimenting with different strength and conditioning exercises, I became able to rep 100 pounds, 100 times, during one set with my bench press. I was also taking judo and had won a few tournaments, earning my brown belt. One time, I remember hearing that my challenger was a hulk of a man, standing 6'3" and weighing 230 pounds. I was 5'10" and 200 pounds. I threw him around the mat like a rag doll…and won the tournament.

I tried downhill skiing, cross country skiing, and salmon fishing, once catching a 23-pound salmon with my uncle and cousins on Lake Michigan. I tried golfing with friends and family. I tried, but was not very good. It was more of a social event than really golfing. We got quite a few laughs back in the day. I quit bowling because I kept throwing the bowling ball into the wrong lane.

Some of my fondest memories from my youth included bonfires during the harsh Michigan winters, and ice skating. We continued our tradition of bonfires and also I learned to skate well again, usually with a sister or aunt guiding me around the lake or pond.

There wasn't anything I thought I could not do. One year, I took my family to Myrtle Beach, South Carolina. My Uncle Glen and I decided to venture out after everyone had gone to bed. We were out to have fun and I had my shirt off as we walked along the beach. We came across a group of young guys drinking on the beach and arm wrestling. Glen spoke up and introduced me as his nephew, "the arm wrestling champion of Michigan." I heard a few snickers as he continued with his proposition: "If Howard can beat all you boys in arm wrestling, we can have some beers with you." We drank until sunrise!

The next day Uncle Glen and I decided to try bumper cars. Evidently, they did not see him help me into my car. I was all over the place, laughing and running into everything and everyone. My knees were bleeding, and finally they stopped the ride and said,

"What are you, blind?" I said, "Why yes, I am!" They kicked us off the ride for safety reasons.

As you can tell, I still had a lot of maturing to do. It is true that I wasn't just sitting around being bitter, a young man defining myself as a victim, but I had not yet done enough character development work that had been absent in my upbringing.

I was not afraid to fight and during my younger years I had my fair share of blind fights, most often winning and hurting others in the process. I am not proud of my fighting and violence during those years. Fortunately, people who were good influences continued to come into my life, and I experienced tremendous personal growth as a result. (The trick is, when they show up, listen!) Again, I am forever grateful that Milt Jo came into my life when he did, and that I took on his attitude of optimism, determination, and self-reliance.

Milt and I continued to stay in touch over the course of several years. One year, he came to Michigan to spend time with my family and me during the Christmas holidays. He sounded weaker than I had ever heard him sound, and I was told he did not look well. Finally, after several days, he requested that we take him to the airport so he could fly back to California to be with his family. He hugged me and said, "Soldier—do not give up. I did!. Never give up!" The next day, our phone rang. It was Milt's family sharing the sad news that Milt passed away during the night. That man left a deep impression in my life—so much so that I later named my daughter Jennifer Jo Myers, in honor of my friend and mentor, Milt Jo.

"There is no passion to be found playing small—in settling for a life that is less than the one you are capable of living."

—*Nelson Mandela*

Chapter 7
Looking for a Job, Finding a Miracle

Milt Jo's admonition to *never give up* resonated with me. The message lodged in my psyche and would *never give up*. It inspired me to find something to apply myself to that would provide me with a purpose. Even with my determination to embrace my new reality and stay positive, it was, and always will be, extremely difficult to fully function in a world designed by and for sighted people.

After coming back from rehab and trying to establish a somewhat normal routine with my family, a sense of frustration began to well up inside me. It felt as if people were treating me differently. I felt like I was being looked at as a pitiful, disabled person, not as the person I believed myself to be. My perception of my new reality made me feel like less of a man. Shame became a constant.

I wanted something to satisfy my inner craving for a larger purpose in life. I knew I was not "useless" but I needed to be fully engaged in useful pursuits, so I began a determined effort to find a job. I had a friend drop me off in town and went from factory to factory hoping for any type of employment. I was willing to do anything, even if it was only putting nuts on bolts.

At home, days seemed endless with a lot of free time on my hands waiting for responses to my job applications. I acted like a caged lion (complete with the occasional roar), alternating between lying around and pacing the floor as best I could in my darkness.

My frustration sprang from two sources. First, I really, really wanted a job. I kept hearing from people who said they wanted to help me, but their help never panned out. "Don't call us," they said, "we'll call you." And somehow that phone would never ring.

My second source of frustration lay deep within me. I was starting to hate myself because of my blindness. Deep down, I was lost. I wanted to find a job where I could have a goal, where I could get excited, and most importantly, where I could feel like a man again and not be that "poor blinded veteran." I just had not been able to find that kind of a job and, I must admit, my attitude was beginning to be quite negative. I fought to stay optimistic and to not give into being a hopeless victim. I really felt that if I could just find a job I would have some purpose, and have my dignity restored.

The longer I let this go on, the more powerless, frustrated, and depressed I felt. But here's the thing: I did not let it continue for long. Everyone goes through periods where things are not clicking, not moving forward, not going the way we want them to go. The all-important key is to catch yourself and decide to make a course correction instead of riding the downward spiral. Yes, it can be that simple—make a decision to intervene in the situation, ask yourself what the next right action would be to change direction, choose to take that action and follow through.

I made a conscious decision to fill up time with exercise. This turned out to be a very smart, healthy, and productive choice, with many short- and long-term benefits. I joined a fitness club which led to connecting with positive people during these early difficult years.

The exercise, combined with the social interaction, was like magic medicine and helped me gain greater confidence. Over time, the men in the fitness club got to know me and respected me for my training and discipline as well as my eagerness to find a job and provide a living for my family. I needed their respect and the process was very therapeutic.

Chapter 7: Looking for a Job, Finding a Miracle

At the time I did not realize what an important decision I had made. When you intervene like that, when you stop a thought-train of negative freight and get yourself on a more positive track, it seems to cause a ripple all around you, and one good thing leads to another. I am reminded of one of my favorite quotes, attributed to a man who made a brave and amazing journey over the Himalayan Mountains.

> "Until one is committed, there is hesitancy, the chance to draw back, always ineffectiveness. Concerning all acts of initiative (and creation), there is one elementary truth, the ignorance of which kills countless ideas and splendid plans: that the moment one definitely commits oneself, then Providence moves too. All sorts of things occur to help one that would never otherwise have occurred. A whole stream of events issues from the decision, raising in one's favour all manner of unforeseen incidents and meetings and material assistance, which no man could have dreamt would have come his way. I have learned a deep respect for one of Goethe's couplets:
>
> 'Whatever you can do, or dream you can, begin it. Boldness has genius, power, and magic in it!'"
>
> —*William Hutchison Murray*

The manager of the fitness club, John, called the local paper to pitch a story about a blinded Vietnam veteran who was seeking a job. The reporter and newspaper photographer came to my home in Davison, Michigan. The photographer captured a picture of me feeding my one-year-old son, Chad.

Howard with one-year-old Chad,
published in The Flint Journal, *December 1968*

The reporter sat down and began asking me a series of questions. *How did you lose your eyesight? Why are you so eager to find a job?*

My responses came not only from my history but also from my heart. I described how I lost my sight in a landmine explosion in Nam and summarized my recovery journey. I explained that my disability compensation from the military was sufficient for our basic family needs, but that my greatest desire was to have a career so I could feel better about myself, make a contribution to our community, and set some goals in my life.

Sitting around is not my idea of living! I went on to say, "I am getting bored. I refuse to sit around and watch TV all day. I NEED something to do." What I now realize is that we all really need a sense of purpose to fully appreciate living.

On the very evening of the day that the article appeared in the newspaper, my phone rang. At the other end of the line was a gentleman by the name of Denny Floden. He identified himself as the Staff Supervisor for Mass Mutual in Flint, Michigan, and that he wanted to discuss the possibility of me becoming one of their insurance agents. My first response was, "I've never heard of your company."

"Don't worry about that," he quickly responded, "They haven't heard of you either."

Denny came over to my house a few days later for the initial interview. I had decided I would take the job if offered since I had not been able to generate other options.

We began to talk and I surmised that Denny had been sincere in offering a job opportunity to me, but that he soon realized he had reacted to the article's introduction of me based on his emotions. As we explored the possibilities of my working with Mass Mutual and becoming a successful life insurance agent, it dawned on him that there were monumental hurdles in my path. For example, the rate book that agents used to calculate premiums was more than three inches thick. Even with good eyesight, everyone had trouble reading the extremely small print. This was before laptop computers were invented and we did not have any of the technology tools that are available today. He felt that I should have a full-time assistant, but he was not in a position to provide one. I sensed he was having second thoughts about hiring me.

I told Denny that everyone who had interviewed me suggested, "Don't call us, we'll call you." But my phone never rang. Denny responded, "You won't have that problem with me. You'll have to call us because I don't think we'll be calling you." And, as graciously as possible, he concluded the interview.

When Denny returned to the office, he told his boss, Joe, about meeting with me and that he felt bad because he had probably given me false hopes. "What should I do now?" Denny asked.

"Well," Joe said, "I guess you better hope he doesn't call."

But I did call. During the interview, I had said that I wanted to "be treated like everyone else, not like a disabled blind guy." So the company proceeded with the usual hiring process and gave me the six pre-contract training books, complete with tests every potential recruit had to complete before they were hired. This process weeded out a lot of people, and Denny admitted later that he thought it would weed out me as well.

Weeks, and then months went by with no follow-up call from me. Denny probably thought he had dodged a bullet—problem solved! But then I finally called and said, "I read the books. What's next?"

Stunned, he suggested I drop by the office and prove that I knew the answers to the test questions. Not only did I know the material, but I would also call out answers even before he finished asking the questions. He blurted out, "How the hell did you get all this information in your head without eyeballs?"

I explained that I took the books to the Federation of the Blind in Flint and had them read the book into a tape recorder; then I listened to the tapes over and over and over. "Unbelievable" was all he uttered as he sat there dumbfounded. "Give me a minute, Howard. I've got to go see the General Agent."

Denny excused himself and went down to Joe's office and asked what he should do next. "What would you normally do at this point?" Joe asked. The look on Joe's face told Denny this was his problem and he had to find the solution. He came back to his office where he had left me and proceeded to call to schedule an exam with the State of Michigan.

I listened as he said, "Hello, I have a young man I would like to schedule for a life, accident, and health insurance exam." He gave my name and social security number. "And one more thing," Denny said, "I need someone to read Mr. Myers' exam questions to him."

I heard the woman respond, "WHAT?"

"I need someone to read Mr. Myers the questions because he is blind."

Her answer was, "We cannot do that!" This was 1969, a long time before the American Disabilities Act was passed in 1990. She went on to say emphatically, "No one, I repeat, no one is allowed in the testing room except the people taking the test and the proctor!"

Then came an interesting response out of Denny—here was his chance to kiss Howard Myers goodbye and be done with this impossible dream, but he didn't. He continued the phone conversation and said, "I want to thank you for your help. You have been very gracious, and I would like to protect you."

She said, "What are you talking about?"

"Before you reject this man," he said, "I think you should go and find out if your boss is prepared to do interviews from every TV station, radio station, and newspaper out of Detroit, Flint, and Lansing, asking why the state of Michigan is denying a Vietnam veteran who gave his eyes fighting for his country the opportunity to take a State of Michigan Insurance Exam."

She called us back in about 90 minutes and informed us, "They think we can make it work." I passed that state exam with a score of 92%.

I went looking for a job and found a miracle.

***

I said I wanted be treated just like everybody else, so Denny did just that—NO SLACK AND NO EXCUSES! I participated in every training that was offered, and, just like everybody else, I was held accountable each week for the number of sales calls, interviews, and closings I made. Denny went on some joint client calls with me for training purposes. It was clear, however, that he was neither my taxi driver nor my secretary, and that if I was to succeed, it would be based on my efforts, not his.

I sometimes wished I hadn't told Denny to treat me like everybody else. He reminded me of my drill sergeant; both were demanding, wouldn't accept excuses, and expected me to do everything right the first time. Denny did have a better sense of humor and a softer voice—most of the time.

Howard at work, Mass Mutual, 1969

We talked about goals and what it would take to be considered successful in my first year. He informed me that the ultimate honor was to be among the "Freshman Five," the top five new Mass Mutual agents in the United States in their first year. "Were you in Freshman Five?" I asked.

He chuckled and said, "No, no one from our office has ever won the Freshman Five Award."

"Good. I'm going to be a Freshman Five, then," I declared. I was the first blind insurance agent in the storied history of Mass Mutual and they did not have averages for blind agents, so I decided to set the mark.

I had a job. I had goals. And, best of all, I had a phenomenal mentor.

***

We all can benefit from coaches and mentors in life and Denny Floden became my mentor. In addition to having a quick wit, he was strong and absolutely determined that both of us would succeed.

We've been friends now for nearly 50 years and still talk frequently, even though we each have gone our separate ways. Over the years, I learned more about the rest of his story and discovered the basis for our connection. As it turned out, I was looking for a job but really found, in a sense, a "brother."

Denny's background was different than mine and he kept it to himself. But over time he opened up and we found we shared some of the same feelings. He had been frustrated, angry, depressed, and confused as a child. You could say that he had a "rather humble childhood." At age 13, he was removed from the care of his mother after a social worker learned he was living in an abusive situation. He went from foster home to foster home as a teenager, and was finally placed in a group living environment at the Children's Aid Society of Indiana.

One day, he was swimming at the YMCA and the lifeguard on duty asked him where he would be attending high school. He said, "Riley High. Why?"

"Come out for the Riley Swim Team," the lifeguard said. "I think I can teach you how to swim better." That man, Dick Fetters, became Denny's coach and mentor—plus the closest thing he ever had to a real father.

Denny didn't know much about his actual father. He said he recalled seeing him around four or five times during his childhood. Like many foster children, he bounced around from house to house, finding the whole foster care process difficult and lonely. Growing up without a stable environment and without the guidance or encouragement of a father or mother, he did not feel that anyone truly believed in him, or that there was anyone who could guide him toward a bright future. That all changed when Denny joined the high school swim team, coached by Dick Fetters.

Coach Fetters was special. He started the Riley High School swim team even though they didn't have a pool at the school. The team practiced at the YMCA in downtown South Bend, Indiana, very early each morning before school. Under Coach Fetters' tutelage, Denny and his teammates won three Indiana State High School Swimming Championships as a team, and Denny won five individual state championships and eventually was inducted into the Indiana High School Swimming Hall of Fame.

Coach Dick Fetters with Denny Floden,
Induction into Riley High School Hall of Fame

Most importantly, the coach *cared* about his athletes and guided them towards becoming responsible and productive young men. He taught more than how to compete; he taught discipline and structure, and how to survive and eventually thrive in sports and in life. He challenged his boys to become better human beings and not to let childhood circumstances stop them from succeeding in any endeavor. Because Coach Fetters believed in Denny, Denny slowly began to believe in himself.

After Denny's junior year, Coach Fetters left Riley High School for a job in Florida. Although his departure left a big void, Coach Fetters remained a reliable and positive influence in Denny's life. To be able to attend college, Denny had to obtain a scholarship or it would be impossible financially. Coach Fetters wrote letters of recommendation on behalf of Denny to universities to help Denny get an athletic scholarship.

Denny's dream came true. After accepting a full-ride athletic scholarship to the University of Michigan, he visited Coach Fetters to thank him for all he had done for him. In his naive exuberance, he told him, "Coach, someday I'm going to be a millionaire and repay you for all you've done for me!"

Coach looked at Denny with his clever smile and said, "If you really want to repay me, just do for someone else what I have tried to do for you. That's the best way to repay anyone."

He followed in Coach Fetters' path and became a swimming coach for a short time. Later, Denny started selling life insurance for Mass Mutual where he met his next mentors, Frank Comins and Joe Shomsky. They picked up where Coach Fetters left off, giving him advice and guidance. They taught him that selling was, or at least should be, about serving and doing what is best for the customer. The motto for Mass Mutual back then was: "We Serve." Joe and Frank lived by that motto. Later, Denny's responsibilities were expanded to recruiting and training life insurance sales agents. That's when he read about me in the local newspaper.

Responding to that article, I wonder if he realized he was about to fulfill on what his mentor, Coach Fetters, had challenged him to do; he was about to make a profound difference in the life of someone who needed him so much, someone who would welcome his guidance and appreciate him as a mentor for life. Even when he pissed me off.

One day I burst into Denny's office—steaming mad, red-faced and pissed off about the Social Security Administration. He attempted to calm me down as best as he could and asked what the problem was. "Those SOBs just cut off my Social Security Benefits," I responded.

"Why?" he asked.

"They say I'm making too much money to be qualified as disabled!"

He paused for a moment, and in a low calm voice asked me, in view of my success, did I still feel that I was truly disabled—and then he reminded me that I "wanted to be treated like everybody else."

I spit out, "You prick," turned, and slammed the door shut behind me as I walked out.

At that moment in time, I stopped focusing on my disability. I started getting rid of "dis" and from then on, stayed focused on "ability." I was no longer a victim of my circumstances. Denny's initial belief in me was the foundation for believing in myself, just as Coach Fetters' belief in Denny was the basis of his self-confidence.

What I was learning was to focus on ability by *visualizing* what I wanted to happen.

Visualizing takes place in your mind and, fortunately for me, can be clear and effective even if you have no eyesight. In fact, I derive a lot of pleasure when I visualize my goals and dreams because this practice takes me out of my dark world and gives me a vivid, uplifting experience. I love my blind vision.

I once read the definition of *worrying* is "to use the power of your mind to imagine what you do NOT want to happen." Instead, use your mind to visualize what you most want, and let go of everything else. Do your best to live in a positive environment, which means choosing not only your surroundings, but also what you train your mind to focus on.

During my career with Mass Mutual, I was blessed to be in a positive environment, surrounded by winners. Every Monday morning, the Mass Mutual agents attended mandatory personal development training in motivation, accountability, and sales development. These sessions were run by Mass Mutual leaders who brought their championship mindsets from the University of Michigan. Frank Comins and Joe Shomsky were the General Agents leading the way. Frank was an older, distinguished gentleman who oozed dignity and leadership. Joe was on the football team at the University of Michigan. Staff Supervisor/Assistant, General Agent Denny Floden was a three-time All-American while part of three consecutive NCAA National Championship Swimming Teams at the University of Michigan. These men mentored me and gave special insight into developing a championship mindset.

I was hungry for success so I followed my mentors' advice and did not overthink things. If I was supposed to make one hundred calls, then I did 101 calls. If I was supposed to listen to motivational material to get in the right mindset, then I did this, too. I was taught that winners do not make excuses. If they want something deeply enough, then they will find a way to achieve it.

Selling life insurance is a tough business. Industry averages show that four out of five people who enter the business do not make it. I was the fifth man. I set lofty goals, reviewed them daily, visualized my success, and set out to reach them with grit and tenacity.

I am often asked how I was so successful at selling. To be honest, I never really thought about selling, I thought about serving. I was providing a service for families. I believed that what I had to share was beneficial for the family's future well-being. I knew that I was simply sharing information and helping them make an informed decision.

Through the process of learning how to operate as a career agent with Mass Mutual, whenever a so-called problem would arise, I didn't focus on the problem, I looked for solutions. I simply used the power of my imagination, got creative, and focused on possibilities. Excuses are just stories we tell ourselves when we take our eyes off of our goals. Also helpful to me was my ability to harness the mental toughness training the military had provided and transfer it into the business world.

To prepare for an appointment, I would review the necessary paperwork, rates and values of the insurance proposal, and focus my mindset on serving the people I was about to meet. Then I had to arrange for a ride either by taxi, colleagues, or I would hire a driver. I would even ask some of my clients after I closed the sale to give me a ride to my next appointment or back to the office.

Once I was in front of a prospect, I would simply say, "May I borrow your eyes for a moment and have you share with me what you see on page three, in column five of the printout?" Once they would read the values, I would punch the figures into my talking calculator and they could hear the outcome. Together, my clients and I worked through the sales process as as partners. Discussing the benefits of the program, building rapport, and finally filling out the applications got the client involved in the process. If there was any selling involved, the clients were selling themselves. Over the years many of my clients have become life-long friends. It really became a process of reciprocity. I was helping them and in turn they were helping me, a genuine win/win relationship.

Again, the key was for me to use my *ability*, not let any "dis" impede me. At times, maybe because I intentionally made things look easy when possible, people would forget I may have needed help out of a car or into a building. One afternoon, Denny and I decided to grab some lunch. He parallel parked his car, proceeded to get out and head into the restaurant leaving me to fend for myself. As he approached the door, he heard a very loud THUD followed by my foul mouth, "You asshole!" As I exited the car, I had walked straight into a light pole and smacked my head hard.

It really hurt as I stumbled around and I bawled out, "Did you forget I was blind, you SOB?"

Denny said, "Howard, as a matter of fact, I did!" After the initial embarrassment and throbbing went away, we laughed. After all, he was honoring my request to be "treated like everyone else, not like a disabled blind guy."

One day, I learned that there was a new business opening up in our area called Dukes and decided to pay them a visit the following week. I had a taxi driver drop me off as I wanted to introduce myself to the new owners. I did not see the sign that said "Fresh Paint" and I brushed up against the walls to help guide me as I banged around looking for someone to introduce myself to. I had just purchased a brand new, brown suede sport coat. Evidently, I smeared fresh white paint on the sleeve as I stumbled in. The new owners felt terrible and tried to get the paint off. Of course I tried to ease the awkwardness of the situation by laughing it off, and we soon were sitting down talking about insurance. Eventually, the owners came to be among one my best clients.

I can guarantee that I have made many mistakes and had lots of failures along the way to success, but I was never afraid to fail. I became immune to the word "No" in sales. Instead of focusing on the "No," I simply focused on the word "Next!"

I experimented with business much like life. I was gaining valuable experience day by day. Failure wasn't my enemy, it was my best teacher!

Each year, Mass Mutual held a prestigious President and Leaders Club Conference. Some time after the fact, I learned that Joe, my General Agent, called Denny into his office, sat him down and looked across the desk, saying, "Do you remember our concerns and uncertainty about hiring a blind guy? Well, you're not going to believe this, but I was just informed by our home office that our very own Howard Myers just received our first ever Freshman Five Award! He finished #2 nationwide out of all rookie agents! He will be honored at the Leaders Club Conference. Denny, I want you to have the honor or calling Howard down to my office so we can share the news."

Denny waltzed down the hall with a smile on his face, much like the smile Coach Fetters wore years ago when encouraging Denny to "pay it forward."

"Howard, Joe wants you in his office immediately!" he said, without a trace of a smile in his voice. I grabbed my cane and asked Denny what was going on. Denny replied, "Joe just wants us in his office right away." I tapped my cane against the walls, down the hall, and into Joe's office, where Denny escorted me into a chair. Joe cleared his throat, "Howard, do you know why we called you to my office today?"

And so, at the age of 23, I was invited to Mass Mutual's President and Leaders Conference in San Juan, Puerto Rico, with my wife Kristi. I was ceremoniously given the National Freshman Five Award, The award recognizes individuals who have achieved the highest levels of all-around sales and service performance in their first year representing Mass Mutual. Today, Mass Mutual has a field of more than 4,000 agents, and still, only five are selected to receive this prestigious award.

What a win for me. What a win for my mentors. What a win for Coach Fetters.

"All relationships are an endless dance of harmony, disharmony and repair."

—*Terry Real*

Chapter 8
For Better or Worse

After I started working at Mass Mutual, I was happy that my professional life was taking off; however, my personal life had taken a disappointing turn. I was still married to my high school sweetheart, Kristi. Adapting to my blindness was a struggle for us both. We were having a difficult time accepting the truth and living with what had happened to me. It must have been incredibly hard for Kristi to accept that the sighted man she had married was now blind. Kristi was a lovely young lady, but her blind husband had lost his ability to stay emotionally connected to her. We struggled to keep the marriage together. In time, we stopped sharing experiences and we stopped growing together as a couple. We drifted apart to the point where we were unfaithful to each other, a fatal blow to our relationship.

Looking back, both Kristi and I were too young, too immature, and neither one of us had any idea about how to keep a family together. Her knight in shining armor, the man who was going to take her away from her horrible life, was now a failure as her spouse.

After I decided to start the process of divorce, I lived with my parents for a short time, then I lived alone in a senior citizen complex for several months. Later, I moved in with Bob Olson, a prior two-time All-American linebacker for the Notre Dame football team and a coworker at Mass Mutual.

Being a young, intrepid risk-taker, I fell into the habit of crazy partying and drinking. I became a house hopper. I never thought about the "how" in life, I just made up my mind and did it. I was a hotshot insurance agent and wasn't afraid to "show off" by having a popular clothing store in Flint, Marvin's, outfit me in colorful, flashy attire.

However, most of the professionals in the Mass Mutual agency wore grey, black, and white. Maybe navy with pinstripes...always conservative. Although some of the agents described me looking like a clown, many of the women thought otherwise. I would strut into the insurance office looking more like a disco dancer than a traditional insurance agent. Can you imagine? I actually wore an electric lime-green leisure suit with my shades to work.

In 1971, while I was working at Mass Mutual, I met a secretary named Debbie who I thought had the voice of an angel. All of the agents had been telling me about this cute little brunette who had a beautiful figure. I got to know Debbie because I had to take my life applications to her, and she would bring memos up to my office and read them to me. What was intriguing to me about Debbie was that she was a great listener. She was quiet and always made me wonder what she was thinking. She seemed to really listen to my comments or stories, responding thoughtfully instead of with a quick, automatic response. I thought I might just give it a try.

Kristi and I had finally decided to divorce, but back then it was not so easy to end a marriage. Since I was technically married at the time, Debbie didn't want anything to do with me. But I was persistent. After pursuing her for more than two years, I finally convinced Debbie to have lunch with me. At this stage in my life, I was keen on dressing to kill to match my success as an insurance agent. It seems she was attracted to that. She didn't know anything about the Freshman Five—but she figured that I was hard working and probably had plenty of money.

Not only were divorce laws back then a lot different than they are today, but so were inter-office romance policies. When my agency managers found out about our lunch dates, they fired Debbie.

I was the salesman and she was simply a secretary. It wasn't fair, but that was life in the seventies.

Debbie found work elsewhere, and we kept dating. I began doing a great deal of public speaking and I invited Debbie to travel with me. Her loyalty became apparent to me as she started to pick up the slack for some of the things that I was not able to do as a blind man, and she has continued to do so over the years of my career.

My divorce was granted in 1973, and Debbie and I married in 1974. Debbie and I lived with her son, Michael, with my children, Chad and Jennifer, visiting occasionally. My children were always on my mind as I knew their mother, Kristi, was with a potentially dangerous man who was verbally, physically and emotionally abusive. Worse yet, they lived hours away on the other side of the state. I recall one day in particular after I had just spent a long weekend with my children. They desperately wanted to live with Debbie and me. Unfortunately, my ex-wife had legal custody. I put Chad and Jennie on the front seat of a Greyhound bus in Flint to return to Grand Rapids, Michigan, where their mother would pick them up at the bus station. I was told where they were seated and I looked up toward the bus window and a few tears rolled down my cheek. Later I was told both my children saw my tears and they wept all the way to Grand Rapids. When they arrived home, my ex-wife's boyfriend asked my son why he was crying. Chad blubbered, "I miss my dad." This man was not aware of how to show compassion for my son but instead he spat out, "If you do not stop crying, I will give you something to cry about!"

Chad shouted back, "You cannot punish me for missing my father!" This only got him a severe beating with a belt. Later, I found out about this episode as I was building up reserves of resentment and bitterness and I knew it was just a matter of time before I was going to have my day.

At this time in my life I was very fit, working out nearly every day. I had 19-inch arms with a huge barrel chest and I was not going to tolerate this insecure, abusive man harming my children. Time and time again I heard stories and I was taking inventory.

Finally, I decided to do something about this. My ex-roommate, Bob (the former linebacker) and I decided to take time off work to find him. We waited in the parking lot and I asked Bob not to get involved, only to squeeze my arm when we were approaching.

When the jerk spotted us, he sarcastically yelled out, "What are you doing here, blind man?" That was all I needed—the sound of his voice! I grabbed hold of him and proceeded to beat him to a pulp. He was able to finally wiggle away and stumble to his vehicle. Today, I can say I am not proud of fighting violence with violence, as this only led to more issues.

That night, my ex-wife called me and said, "Thanks, Howard, I just got my ass kicked by Terry because of you!" A few weeks later, I came to pick up my children and I was told he came to the door with a butcher knife hidden behind his back in case I wanted to start something. This kind of lifestyle is absolutely insane and I was not aware at the time of how I attracted this type of behavior. I had solved most of my problems in life with money, violence, control and charm. However, none of these tactics could save my children.

One morning my phone rang at the office. On the other end of the phone was the distraught voice of my ex-wife, Kristi. She explained that she needed to drop off our children at my office. She had left her home in Grand Rapids, Michigan, in the middle of the night to escape the abuse. She was tired, desperate and wanted what was best for our kids.

Later I found out that the previous night Kristi had been the victim of severe abuse. Chad and Jennie were told everything was going to be okay and they were sent to bed and instructed not to get up. Early the next morning, Kristi told her children to quickly grab a few personal belongings and some clothes and to go to the car immediately. I also found out that she did not have any cash or credit cards so she had to sell a lamp to the neighbor for gas money as her car was on empty. My son told me his mother was very frightened and had a black eye. She obviously had not slept the night before as she waited for Terry to leave for work to make her escape with her children. Chad also told me he was on high alert, looking out the back window of his mother's car, watching for Terry. It was obvious my children and ex-wife were living in a state of fear on a daily basis. Finally Kristi knew it was time to get her children out of this destructive and dangerous environment. Kristi tried to drive across the state without any sleep but finally succumbed to exhaustion and pulled over at a rest area to sleep. She assured our children they were safe yet Chad was not buying it; he stayed on alert, on the lookout for anything suspicious, until his mother awoke. Finally Kristi arrived at my Mass Mutual office in Flint. My coworkers described her as someone who looked like she had just been through a war.

This was the third emergency drop-off and I was about to receive custody of Jen and Chad. She dropped the kids off at 10 a.m.—by 4 p.m., I had full custody of my son and daughter. My attorney Del Green was able to draw up the paperwork and I caught my ex-wife at a weak moment and she signed the papers. I believe this was the most difficult thing a mother could do but she knew they were better off at the time as she needed to run and hide. My children were very happy to be with me but little did I know how the past events would affect them during the rest of their childhood.

When Chad and Jennie came to live with Debbie and me, Mike was just turning five years old. As Debbie says, I brought my children home and emphatically said that my children were living with us from now on. Newly married, we now went from a family of three to a family of five overnight.

As we tried settling in with our new family arrangement, I was not aware of the healing my children needed. My children constantly asked about their mother! Where she was living? Was she okay? Could they talk to her? My ex-wife was on the run and left the state out of fear for her life. Debbie and I knew we had to provide a stable environment for our children. We had family breakfasts and dinners, and I tucked my children into bed each night, got down on my knees and prayed for answers. Chad and Jen were recovering from abuse and trauma and I was not sure if I had the knowledge or the tools to help them. Little did I know that I was caught in a trap of shame, grandiosity, charm, ego and competition. The emotional consequences of my childhood programming and war were now affecting my family. I was excelling at being a successful businessman, yet I had a great deal to learn about intimacy, vulnerability and true love. I was kicking ass in my professional world but felt like a failure in my personal life. Like many men, I buried my pain in my work life. Maybe I was a workaholic.

My children were constantly disappointed as they longed to see their mother who continued to stay in hiding, most of the time outside the state of Michigan.

Debbie and I, now married for nearly two years, got some joyful news. Debbie was pregnant. Unfortunately, Debbie went into labor far too early. Our baby girl, Sara, was born at 28 weeks, weighing only 1 pound, 15 ounces. It was 1976 and the doctors and hospital did all they could trying to keep life in our child's lungs and keep her little heart beating. After only six days, our little angel left us and created a larger gap of intimacy between Debbie and me. Debbie rocked Sara after she passed, and as only a mother can, she said good-bye to her daughter.

Being ignorant and often emotionally distant, I attempted to get my needs met in my business world, and with my exercising, my fun, my friends. I was not emotionally supportive of Debbie in the loss of our daughter. I lacked empathy, compassion and wisdom.

To complicate matters even more, our phone rang in the middle of the night informing us that my ex-wife Kristi was in the hospital, barely holding on to her life. It was her birthday, she was out, and her car stalled on the expressway during a cold snowy night in Michigan. She waved a car down, dashed across the expressway, and was struck by a car. Her chance of survival was low.

The next morning we sat our children down and informed them that their mother was in the hospital after being hit by a car. I called Kristi's father who resided in Delaware and he flew to Michigan. I arranged for a ride to the hospital to assess the situation. Again, unaware and unskilled, I was not able to properly be a man and be strong emotionally for my family.

My children's mother, over time, came out of her coma and began slowly recovering. During that time, I tried to reassure my children their mother would be okay, but looking back, I can realize that a few words and a patronizing pat on the back were not nearly sufficient as my children tried to process all that was upside-down in their world.

I continued to perform at high levels professionally, but personally I was not emotionally mature enough to handle all that was coming at me. With my ex-wife recovering from a near fatal accident, and my current wife recovering from the death of our daughter and postpartum depression, I checked out. I buried my emotions in work, play, exercise, and alcohol. I lacked the maturity to provide emotional support for my wife and children.

Debbie picked up where I dropped the responsibilities. I was not much of a team player in my home. Like some men, I felt my role was to be the financial provider, but what my wife and children needed was my presence and emotional support. My children, Chad and Jennifer, had moved far too many times and needed stability, structure, safety, belonging and love. Debbie was strong enough to move through her grief over losing a child, and proceed to step up and be a supportive mother to the children. With or without me, she went to the teacher and school booster meetings, brought the kids to extra-curricular events, sporting events, volunteered at school events, and much more.

After losing our Sara, Debbie and I began to discuss the possibility of trying again to have another child. We decided to expand the family and our son, Joshua Lee Myers, was born on October 10, 1978, weighing only 3 pounds, and was 16 inches long. He had big blue eyes and blonde hair. Finally after five weeks in neo-natal intensive care, he was strong enough to come home. Everyone wanted a baby brother. Josh not only brought Debbie and I closer together, he brought the entire family closer together.

Over the years I have wondered why. What caused Debbie to step in and step up? She simply stated to me, "This is what a mom does!" She went on to say, "I stayed because I knew the children would have suffered." She reminded me about the sadness of my children waiting for their mom, Kristi, on the front porch—she would often not show up when she was running from herself and her former life. With the support of Debbie on the home front, I was able to continue my quest for more and more success in the business world.

Prior to having Debbie's help, I hired many different helpers. They made phone calls, contacted other associates, set up appointments, and assisted with transportation. They even did simple things like playing back voice memos and writing down my thoughts. Unfortunately, many were not very passionate about the work. Debbie, on the other hand, knew what my needs were and supported me the best she could. It was so helpful to me when she finished what I couldn't get others to do. She stepped into the process and took on all of the responsibilities of being a wife, mother, secretary and much more. Debbie gave up on a lot of her dreams so I could continue to pursue mine.

As a younger man, I was not aware of the maturation process I had to endure. I purposely use the word "process" as I now know there really is no finish line. By the grace of God, I finally started to shift my focus from myself and my own gratification to attending to my family. The light in my personal life was becoming brighter. I soon realized that it was my duty as a man to become the emotional regulator of my family. As successful as I was in the professional world, I wanted to experience the same success in my home. Over time, my family life became richer, more satisfying. It was far from perfect, yet my maturity and dedication to my family slowly began to solidify my character. The darkness of my earlier programming as a young boy, along with war and the loss of my eyesight, were very disruptive experiences. Disruptive experiences—toxic or abusive relationships, divorce, death of a loved one, loss of a job, loss of health, a disability, loss of hope— can bring internal responses of habitual anger, anxiety, shame, depression, which in turn change the circuitry and functioning of the brain.

Because of my association with my consulting-group colleagues from the Mindworks Performance Group, I have learned about neuroplasticity, the mind's ability to change the brain. I was learning to live in the light in my personal life, exchanging my darkness for light, by focusing on what I wanted in my life. We can all *choose* empathy, nurturing, positive social connections, rewarding accomplishments, purpose, kindness, compassion, mindfulness, gratitude, generosity, love, awe, contribution, and healing; all of these, in turn, change the circuitry and functioning of the brain.

I became more aware of the fact that who we are and how we cope is not our fault. But in empowering ourselves, especially with the power of *choice,* then who we are and how we cope becomes our responsibility. I was moving away from being a *victim* to learning how to take *responsibility*…and rewriting my family legacy.

Not only did my quality of family life improve, so did my ex-wife, Kristi. After months of recovery from her near-fatal accident, she exchanged her life of fear and running to love and embracing faith. She anchored herself in spirituality, stopped dating, and focused on the healing of her mind, body and soul. She eventually remarried and has been with her husband for the past 37 years, now residing in Florida, enjoying retirement. She shares that it was the grace of God that spared her life.

Debbie and I have been married for 44 years, and I am proud to say that we have been able to work through our shortcomings and stay together. I never had enough sense when I was younger to know how to treat a lady. My early role models and youthful experiences with womanizing did not give me much to go on. I never had enough sense to know what a good husband should be doing until later in life. It was only then that I asked for forgiveness and decided to treat my wife the way she deserved to be treated. What I learned from Debbie is the power of loyalty. She was always there, and still is. I love her more today than I ever have and I am thankful that we are still have one another.

Debbie always accepted me, Howard Myers, "as is," and never tried to change me one bit. That is *loving unconditionally* at its finest. It's the way God loves us, and it took me many years to figure this out.

I have received numerous awards and have achieved a great deal of success in the insurance industry. Looking back on my life, I see that so many things would not have been possible without this wonderful lady who was always there beside me. She has never received the recognition that she deserves. I wouldn't trade her for the world. Debbie says that I am an ordinary man who chooses to do extra-ordinary things. She says that I am the love of her life, her best friend and partner. Certainly that is how I think of her, with gratitude.

Howard and Debbie, wedding day (March 24, 1974)

"Son, be careful where you walk."
" Father, you be careful—remember that I follow your steps."

Author unknown

Chapter 9
Lessons My Children Taught Me

One morning my son Chad approached me when I was in the living room listening to some audio programs. He became quite curious, as the voices emanating from my cassette player sounded enthusiastic and full of life. My son asked me what I was doing. "I am listening to some motivational material to help me keep a positive attitude," I shared.

Over the years, my son was drawn to this regular activity. He would sit down with me and listen for a few moments at a time. It was not until Chad was much older that he realized that this routine of mine was the foundation of much of my success. I was reprogramming my mind each morning, much like the military had programmed me (through repetitive messaging) for war. The great voices of Earl Nightingale, Zig Ziglar, and Wayne Dyer repeated and reinforced how to develop and keep a positive mindset. Over the years, these became ingrained in my psyche:

> "You can have everything in life you want, if you will just help enough other people get what they want." —Zig Ziglar

> "People often say that motivation doesn't last. Well, neither does bathing—that's why we recommend it daily." —Zig Ziglar

> "Whatever we plant in our subconscious mind and nourish with repetition and emotion will one day become a reality."　　　—Earl Nightengale

> "Our environment, the world in which we live and work, is a mirror of our attitudes and expectations."　　　—Earl Nightengale

> "If you change the way you look at things, the things you look at change."　　　—Wayne Dyer

> "How people treat you is their karma; how you react is yours."　　　—Wayne Dyer

> "When you judge another, you do not define them, you define yourself."　　　—Wayne Dyer

My young son, who had recently come from an environment of fear and anxiety, found these affirmations to be meaningful, even exciting. Today, I know that these great voices also became part of him.

Perseverance was another key to my success. Whether it was selling life insurance, becoming the first blind runner in the Crim 10-mile race, or learning to water ski as a blind man, I never stopped trying. I learned quickly that failure is not the opposite of success—it is part of success. We all learn more from failure than success because the challenges in life cause us to grow.

Ironically, at times I made life look easy. I rarely complained, made excuses, or blamed others. I lived above my circumstances and refused to make excuses. The last thing I ever wanted was to appear "needy" or "incapable." The more I acted self-reliant and confident, the more I actually was.

Children are naturally curious and want to explore life through play. My children reminded me that it is okay to play hard, to use my imagination, and be creative. One of Chad's first words spoken was "ball." I remember coming home one day and heard my son say he wanted to go out for the youth football team. I figured that playing catch with my son was something I had to learn how to do regardless of sight. An idea flashed into my mind. I told my son to grab the football and guide me to our backyard. I then told him to run out and call out, "Right here." He did so, and I asked, "Where?" When he repeated, "Right here," I threw the ball toward his voice, and he caught the ball. Amazed at our success, he ran back to me, gave me the ball, and we did it again and again. As I tossed him the ball I would share stories of my sighted days, of being an athlete in high school.

I learned that the less I gave advice and the more I led by example, the better. I knew the positive effects of exercise in my life yet little did I know that exercise over the years would be a crucial source for my well-being. As mentioned in an earlier chapter, I worked out several times a week at a local fitness club. At the time, Chad was 12 years old, and boys were not allowed at my gym. However, I was persistent, and I somehow convinced the club manager to give my son a membership, claiming I needed assistance around the gym. Everyone knew this was not true, as I had been working out there for over twelve years without my son, but the result was that I was able to introduce the world of fitness and exercise to him.

My children reminded me that they will mirror their parents, both our strengths and weaknesses. I would challenge my son to do more push-ups and more sit-ups than me. The military training and mental toughness was how I was wired and I was able to pass this on to my sons. Most of the time I was able to be a good role model by being active and healthy. Looking back, it is easy to see some of the positive programming. Those days at the gym gave my sons purpose and kept them out of trouble as young men.

Chad tried nearly every sport at school, including track, baseball, football and basketball. One year, when he was running track, I shared an old memory, "I believed I could run faster than anyone, and I did, most of the time."

I ran the quarter-mile in high school and held the school record for years in this event. I was proud that Chad was running the same event. I said, "Get behind the fastest runner and allow them to set the pace for the race and when you come around the last turn, explode and burst past him!" Most of the time he did run faster than his competition.

My children reminded me that regardless of sight, it was my presence that mattered most. I rarely, if ever, made excuses to not support my children's interest, no matter what sporting event they participated in, my children could look towards the sidelines, up in the bleachers, or towards the fence, and I was almost always there. I would ask my wife, friends, business colleagues, or relatives to take me to my children's events and be my eyes. They would describe as much as possible the play-by-play of the game or my daughter Jennie cheerleading on the sidelines.

Like father, like son. One evening during Chad's opening basketball game of his senior season, I called the school office. He was attending school nearly an hour away from where I was, and I had not been able to find a ride to the game. "I'm just not going to be able to make it tonight," I said with great disappointment.

"Dad, that's okay," Chad said. "You have made it to nearly all my games. I am dedicating this game to you and guaranteeing a win!"

The year before, the opponents punished his school by over 40 points. This go-round was going to be different. From the opening tip-off, the teams battled back and forth, and half-time found the opponents stunned: his team was in the lead! Chad went on to share with me the following: "For whatever reason, I was in the zone. I simply could not miss." At the end of the game, with only a few moments to play, he stole the ball, dashed to our basket and was shoved into the wall as he banked the ball in. The opposing player was ejected for a flagrant foul and Chad was given the chance to sink two free throws. He did his usual three dribbles, took a deep breath, and sank both free throws.

His opponents made a desperate attempt and nearly hit the last shot from half court, but at the end the scoreboard flashed 73 to 72. His team had won, and my son had scored 46 points (and this was before the 3-point line was implemented). He screamed into the phone, "We won by one point and I scored 46 points!" On the other end of the phone, I sat and listened with great joy and even shed a tear. For many years my son held the scoring record at his school; he was featured in the local newspaper, often leading the county in scoring and making the all-county dream team.

Of course, as parents, often we do not realize how important it is for our children to have us present with them when they are experimenting with different activities and extra-curricular events. Being at my children's sporting events allowed me to support them and, in turn, they gave me the joy of enjoying them. Parenting is a privilege, a responsibility, and an honor for me.

My children also reminded me to be adventurous and explore the unknown. One particular Saturday morning I knocked on Chad's bedroom door and asked him if he wanted to learn how to drive. He sarcastically said, "Who is going to teach me?"

I retorted, "I am!"

"Excuse me? But dad, I have never driven and you are blind!" I reassured him that I knew exactly how to teach him to drive and how to navigate, so the two of us could visit relatives and friends. I was going to be the copilot: truly the blind leading the ignorant. Without a single driver's training class under his belt or a sighted passenger, he decided to drive.

My son would later discover that I started when I was 12, driving alone down dirt roads when working on a farm. I had enough years under my belt before losing my sight that I could confidently instruct Chad on driving. This was not just a lesson in driving but it became a day of lessons of life, as many of our drives became over the years. Before we left the driveway I gave my discourse on safety and responsibility. I explained it was a privilege to drive, but it is also a responsibility to others and yourself to be a good driver. We went over the basics of driving and, before I knew it, Chad put the car in reverse, looked over his right shoulder and backed out of the driveway onto Sunnymead Drive, and proceeded to cruise the main roads toward my parents' home. This was an unexpected visit and, to say the least, they were very surprised when they observed we were alone. We left after a few lectures from my mother and her famous words, "Lord, have mercy."

This was only the first stop of many. We proceeded toward the country roads where I grew up. I guided my son with my internal GPS. I had created neuronal maps in my brain based on my young life, when I could see, the repetition of being on these roads. That day we did not need a road map. I had one in my head.

My son and I have driven together for years, and we make a good team. I can identify where the roads are by merely feeling and sensing the miles driven and time elapsed. I can identify with great accuracy the name of the road we may have passed or state at a stop sign the name of the road without seeing it. I guess I have always taken this ability for granted.

During that first team drive, Chad was hesitant to tell me we were running out of gas but we could not travel much further without stopping for fuel. Pulling into the gas station for the first time made him nervous. He was most likely stressed and nearly hit the gas pump when trying to pull up for a refill. I imagined the newspaper the next day—blind father and son run into gas pump! I didn't get upset. I did not lecture him. I calmed him down and said we all make mistakes. I reassured him that everything will be fine. At the time I did not understand the significance of how I handled this situation but it gave him the confidence to keep driving.

The rest of the day was like a dream. He started to regain his confidence as he eased up to each stop sign, looked carefully, then slowly took off again. I guided him to the roads I grew up on when I was a teenager. We rolled the windows down on country dirt roads I had traveled on while sighted. It was a beautiful, late spring day. I remember the sun was shining and the skies were blue. I wanted to get Chad on the dirt roads to gain some confidence as a driver. I loved the fresh country air, the familiar smells, the sense of freedom in going just where I had a whim to go, with Chad as my eyes, hands and feet. There was plenty of time for my stories, too.

"Did I ever tell you about the time I drove blind through downtown Lapeer during a car cruise?"

"No, what are you talking about?"

"When I left for Nam, I had a 1964 Plymouth Fury and it was one of my favorite cars I've ever owned. I polished it up every weekend and cruised around different towns before I left for Vietnam. After I lost my eyesight, I talked your mother and some of our friends into driving me around in my car so I could experience "the cruise" again. I would gaze out the passenger window, remembering in detail what downtown Lapeer looked like. I imagined seeing all the cars I used to admire at "the cruise," the girls walking around town, nodding at friends, and feeling proud of myself for working so hard and feeling proud to have bought this car on my own.

Finally, I could not take it anymore. I decided to drive my own damn car and I talked a friend of mine into letting me drive. My high school friend, Lloyd Lake, sat in the passenger seat and grabbed the bottom of the steering wheel as I sat in the driver's seat working the gas, brakes and shifting the gears and pretending to steer. It was a great memory as I did my best to see again as a blind man. As we drove through the city of Lapeer, I vividly recall Lloyd saying, "Howard, the police are on your left." I proceeded to stick my hand out the window and wave at the police officers with a grin on my face and drove on down the road.

As my son and I continued driving down some of the same roads I had driven, I said, "The next road is Lake Pleasant Road. I used to drag race the quarter-mile with my '64 Plymouth Fury 4-on-the-floor when I could see. After I lost my sight, I talked some of my buddies into helping me drag race again. I did the gas and shifting from the driver's seat and friends would steer from the passenger seat at high speeds. I was crazy at times!" I imagine he just shook his head in disbelief.

I remembered driving blind another time. I had been dropped off at the Paddock Lounge where I ran into an old friend, Jim Holt. After I had a few drinks, he offered to give me a ride home. As we walked to the parking lot, I asked if I could drive his car. With only his left hand steering, I drove his classic Corvette home on highway M-15, mashing on the gas pedal and bringing the car to over 100 mph. I drove all the way home. It was about a 30-minute drive. I was braking at each stop sign, then taking off again like a fool, but I was alive and experiencing life. I could feel the engine vibrate and hear the roar of the motor as I revved up the rpm's.

As the stories continued, Chad was driving without any fear and he began to feel grown-up and proud. We traveled to my brother's and sisters' homes and to my old high school, downtown North Branch. I would point out the window toward buildings and, as we passed them, I would name them with eerie accuracy. We even turned up the radio with the windows down and cruised around town. We traveled all day together laughing, sharing stories, and bonding just like any other son and father, sighted or not.

That day, metaphorically speaking, I was "seeing" and living in the light. The connections I have with others are vital; they allow me to see through their eyes. I wake up to see sameness, blackness, darkness, nothingness. But when someone takes the time to describe a person in detail, or the image of towering sunflowers stretching towards the sun, swaying in the breeze against the cornflower blue sky, it allows me to capture that image in my mind and for a time I can see, using "mind sight."

Over the years, I occasionally drive—I get by with a little help from my friends. We find a very deserted road and I drive, all by myself, while someone drives behind me, just in case. I often swerve a little just to feel the road; hopefully no one passes by and thinks I'm a drunk driver! Nope, just a blind one. My latest driving adventure was with my nephew, Lee Myers. We shared the experience of my taking my 1997 Silver Anniversary Edition Corvette out joy riding, reaching nearly 100 mph, as we found a road less traveled. If you happen to see a blind man driving around town, do not be alarmed; I have been driving for years with a perfect driving record.

My children have taught me the importance of inspiration. I was not setting out to inspire, I was simply doing what I thought was healthy for myself, despite my disability, by focusing on my abilities and in the process, setting an example. We must always remember that our actions, good or bad, have a significant ripple effect.

All are grown now, but will always be my precious children, and I continue to learn from them. My son, Joshua, is a hard-working paramedic in the ER of a hospital, and a single father of his son, Grayson. Much like his mother, he is loyal, faithful and an outstanding parent. He is a role model, being present and active in his son's life and providing a stable home. Debbie and I could not be more proud of our son, Josh.

Michael, my adopted son, has always been a faithful father to his children, Abby, Haley and Justin. Again, I attribute his success and loyalty as a father to my wife Debbie.

My son, Chad Myers, began his career in both inner-city and suburban schools as an outside-of-the-box educator whose mission was to empower students to seize the day and live extraordinary lives. Chad motivated students to learn to think and listen to what is within rather than telling them what to think. He has been likened to John Keating (Robin Williams) from the movie, *Dead Poets Society*. He recently worked in Europe with Mindvalley and a group of dedicated parents to help develop an experimental school in Barcelona, Spain, teaching concepts not taught in traditional education.

Chad is also a dedicated, single father raising his son, Cameron. As a father, he coached his son's youth sports, and helped guide him by applying some of the mentoring I was so fortunate to be blessed with and then passed on to Chad. My grandson, Cameron, recently shared how grateful he was for the legacy funneled down, starting with Coach Fetters, through Denny Floden, myself, and his father.

The same championship mindset brought from the Mass Mutual office in the late 60's and early 70's has influenced my grandson in ways I cannot articulate. As a young man of 26 years of age, he is a serial entrepreneur owning Cam Myers Digital Marketing in Traverse City, Michigan. It is a reminder that what we do speaks so loudly to our children and grandchildren.

My daughter, Jennifer Jo, learned that her son Austin was diagnosed with autism at the age of four. She became a warrior, staying strong for her child and for herself. She later took that strength and used it to found and build Inspiring Hearts for Autism (IHA), a non-profit organization designed to improve the lives of those people touched personally by autism.

Her IHA journey began with a support group held in her own home, and that blossomed into countless hours of consultations and meetings, advocating for autistic kids and parents at schools, advocating at City Hall to have April recognized as Autism Awareness Month, and training and educating local emergency personnel. Jennifer pioneered a business plan for an autism center through Community Mental Health, seeking donations and making a presentation locally to Lt. Gov. Brian Calley in 2014.

After more than a decade, she decided to pass the torch, step down, and move in another direction for herself. In an interview for the newspaper, she said, "The most important thing has been linking families, allowing them to feel understood and reminded they are not alone, providing lifelong friendships and camaraderie. The focus has been and continues to be enriching and empowering the lives of the kids and families who face autism daily."

It is with much gratitude (and pride) that I see that all of our children are becoming more supportive, passionate, emotionally-responsible parents. These developing parenthood traits will hopefully benefit my grandchildren, great-grandchildren, and all future generations. It is my intention and goal—even at the age of 72—to continue to improve and grow for my family's sake, always keeping in mind the ripple effect.

As author Terry Real writes, "In a family, the roles we pass from generation to generation can be like a fire in the woods, taking down everything in its path until one person has the courage to stand and face the fire. That fire is the legacy of esteem for oneself and for others that is learned from the family dynamic…. The best gift you can give your children is a healthier you."

Joshua Myers, Howard Myers, Chad Myers,
Jennifer Myers, Michael Myers
45 years after Howard received his Purple Heart (2012)

Howard teaches Chad (aged 9)
to look in the mirror while shaving

Jennifer (aged 7) and Howard

Joshua and Howard at one of their workouts together

Howard and Jennifer, Thanksgiving, 2008

Jennifer, Howard and Chad
Inspiring Hearts for Autism, 2012

Chad and Howard
Training for the Crim Festival of Races (2013)

Cameron with his dad (Chad) and grandfather (Howard)
at Howard's alma mater, North Branch High School,
as honorary game captain and half-time speaker (2007)

"Independence is the outstanding characteristic of the runner."

—Noel Carroll

Chapter 10
The Sound of Footsteps

Blindness has taught me many beautiful lessons in life. One lesson is that we often take many of the privileges we have for granted; for example, the privileges of walking, running, and exercising. So many have these privileges yet so many are not taking advantage of their God-given abilities. When I was in high school I loved to run, setting records in track and scoring touchdowns in football. I would run like the wind. After I lost my sight, I realized running again may be nearly impossible. Yet I never gave up hope. As a matter of fact, I began believing that I could run again.

John Foguth, a career agent with Mass Mutual and an avid runner who could run a 10-mile race in under 60 minutes, asked me if I was interested in running with him. He attempted to teach me how to run as a blind man, and I learned to follow a sighted runner by listening to his voice and footsteps.

In time, I began to gain some confidence in running as I practiced with John. After some time, I decided that I was going to run the "Crim," a 10-mile race that is locally very popular. I decided to contact Lois Craig, the Crim director, to see if the officials would allow a blind man to enter.

The Crim race began in 1976 when Bobby D. Crim, Speaker of the House, Michigan House of Representatives, was invited to attend a sporting event for a new organization called the "Special Olympics." Bobby had run track when he was in high school and he returned to the sport for health reasons, to help him with his

97

smoking problem and with his weight gain. After Bobby saw his first Special Olympics, Bobby was so impressed with the organization that he wanted to find a way to help. That's how the Crim race was born. Originally intended to be a one-time race to raise $10,000 for the Special Olympics, the Crim 10-Mile Road Race attracted over 700 runners and raised over $36,000 for the Special Olympics.

Over the years, the Crim Festival of Races has attracted world class runners from all over the planet. It has been held now for decades and I hope it continues, as it has raised millions of dollars for the cause. The Crim Festival of Races has expanded into the Crim Fitness Foundation serving the greater Flint area by encouraging people to adopt healthy lifestyles by integrating physical activity, healthy eating, and mindfulness into their daily lives, and mentors other communities to do the same.

I called the director, Lois Craig, in 1982 and told her that I was a blind Vietnam vet and I wanted to run the Crim. I explained how I would run tethered to the wrist of Bobby Crim, who could direct me verbally about any problems—such as curbs, potholes and other potential obstacles in the road. At first, Lois was at a loss for words. Bobby was a competitive runner who wanted to register a strong time in the Crim, but I was determined I could run with several thousand other runners. And to secure my spot, I had found a businessman who donated a couple of thousand dollars in pledges.

I began my quest to prepare for my first race. Determined to find a way, I was able to create a network of runners far and wide to help train me to run 10-miles in total darkness. On days where I could not train, my wife Debbie or I hired help to drive the car down dirt roads or roads less traveled where I would grasp hold of the side view mirror and jog. This took deep trust on my part but I desired to run more than I cared about my fears.

One particular driver would celebrate by drinking a beer for each mile I ran. After I ran 6 miles I began to feel nervous knowing he just finished off a 6-pack of beer. I reminded myself we were only traveling 5 mph or less, but still... At times my wife Debbie would turn up the music in the car and smoke cigarettes while I ran. I would utilize any means possible—high school runners, Crim runners, business colleagues, friends, family—anyone with a pulse became a potential training partner.

At the time, Bobby Crim was the Speaker of the House for the State of Michigan, thus his schedule would not allow him to train with me until a few days before the actual race. On race day, I tethered myself to the founder of the Crim with a strap. I held on to one end, Bobby held on to the other end. I had to let go and trust the process in the midst of thousands of runners for the pure joy of running. We were allowed to start the race 20 minutes early, along with the wheelchair racers and before the mass of typical runners and the world-class runners who can nearly sprint through the whole 10-mile race—the best athletes running under-5-minute miles.

As we began our campaign through the 10-mile race, I was amazed at how fast the world class runners caught up to us. Like a strong breeze, runners from all over the world blasted past us, shouting out words of encouragement to me. More and more runners began approaching us as we moved through the grueling Bradley Hills, patting Bobby and me on the back and encouraging me to keep going in the muggy heat.

Lumbering down Main Street, weary, exhausted, and drenched in perspiration, I could hear the voices, shout-outs, and cheers from the thousands of spectators on the sidewalks of downtown Flint, allowing me to find my last wind and burst of energy! When we finally crossed the finish line, I collapsed into Bobby Crim's arms. We were escorted to a local news crew where we were asked to describe how we were able to maneuver through the sea of runners and conquer the 10-mile race. I shared during the interview that I felt great until the 6- and 7-mile mark and the heat started to overcome me, but Bobby had reassured me—"you got this, Howard"—and his words of encouragement allowed me to gut out the final three miles.

Howard Myers and Bobby Crim
after their first 10-mile race together

Bobby shared during the interview that I inspired him and many others. "It has been our biggest race to date in people and raising money, and it is a privilege for me running with a guy like Howard Myers."

After my first race with Bobby Crim, our relationship continued. One year I challenged Bobby to race me while wearing a blindfold. The loser had to donate $1000 to the Special Olympics. Bobby accepted my challenge and began training with State Representative Bob Emerson. After the race, Bobby admitted that it was by far one of most difficult challenges he endured in his life. Several times he wanted to pull the blindfold off because he found trusting his running partner to maneuver around the potholes, other runners, and vehicles was a real challenge. Despite his blindfold, Bobby (a much trimmer and more experienced runner than me) crossed the finish line well before I was able to with my guide. Bobby told me that as soon as he crossed the finish line he ripped off his blindfold. "This was just a race and my blindness was temporary," he said after the experience. "I cannot even image living in darkness on a daily basis. I gained a whole new respect for Howard Myers and others who have to overcome their disability on a daily basis. I do not know how he does it!"

*Howard Myers, Bobby Crim and Senator Bob Emerson,
just after crossing finish line of the Crim*

Over the years, I have raced in over 50 road races. About 25 of those competitions were in the Crim. My relationship with the Crim has been very special to me. I have been included in special media events and dinners with my good friend Bobby Crim, and have met world-class runners from all over the world. It has been a privilege to be associated with such an incredible organization. Bobby has inspired me in so many ways, and I believe I have done the same for him.

The 40th anniversary of the Crim race was a very special year for me. Bobby Crim and I decided to run the race again together. I was training for the 10-mile race, but that year I suffered a number of injuries and had been sent to rehab for leg and lower back issues. Despite those setbacks, I refused to give up on running. After several months in rehabilitation, I realized that I would have to run the 5K instead. My body would just not tolerate 10 miles of pounding on the pavement.

After Bobby and I committed to running the 5K, he came out to my home with a reporter from ABC 12, a local news station, to do a story about our relationship with each other and running. I led the camera crew and Bobby Crim to my quarter-mile track in the middle of my property where I often run alone. My next-door neighbor, another Vietnam veteran, had created this track for me to run on. In the center of the dirt track is a tall pole with a swivel anchor on top from which a long nylon wire extends to the edge of the track. On the end of the wire is a handle. I simply grab the handle, pull the wire tight and trust the process. As long as I keep tension on the wire I am able to run around my track alone.

I had been *visualizing* being able to run alone for years, but I could not conceive how I might make that happen. One day my neighbor came over, knocked on my door, and asked me to come with him. I wasn't sure what to think, because we had not always gotten along very well. But I allowed him to guide me to this makeshift track. I was quite shocked at the simplicity of the system he had developed to allow me to run independently. Something I had prayed and visualized for years had finally manifested!

The day Bobby and the news crew came out, Bobby wanted to experience what it was like for me to run alone on the track. The camera crew filmed him running for a quarter-mile with his eyes closed. Bobby also wanted to experience what it was like for me to get around my property with my cane. He gave it a go and tapped his way around my sidewalks and the driveway leading to my porch where we conducted an interview with ABC 12. It was the 40th anniversary of the race and our friendship.

That year, after Bobby ran the 10-mile race, he joined me at the starting line for the 5K and we ran alongside my son, Chad, his fiancée, Joanna, and our family friend, Chris Veihl. They all sported Blind Vision shirts. We crossed the finish line with thousands cheering us on, much like they had done during our first race in 1983. The founder of the race, the former Michigan Speaker of the House, and I ran alongside one another, a reminder that anyone can do anything if they set their minds to it. If an 85-year-old retired politician and a 70-year-old blind guy can run against the odds, then we hope we are inspiring others to do the same.

As a result of my running career, I was inducted into the Crim Hall of Fame 2002. I was nominated and received the Governor's Award for Amateur Athletes that same year.

Howard's track at home, where he can run by himself
with his guide line, or with a friend –
pictured here, Howard and Bobby training together
before the 40th anniversary Crim race

Howard and Bobby, triumphant, cross finish line, 40th anniversary Crim race (2016)

Joanna and Chad, Crim Festival of Races (2016)

Chris Veihl, Jennifer Myers, Howard Myers, Joanna Wnuk, Chad Myers (2016)

"Challenges are what make life interesting and overcoming them is what makes life meaningful."

—Joshua Marine

Chapter 11
Finding My Voice

"Everything is created twice, first in the mind and then in reality." (Robin S. Sharma)

Over the years my children and grandchildren visited my home in the country to enjoy the park-like atmosphere I first visualized, then created.

Because I believe that physical exercise is what helped me through life, especially after being blinded, I had to be able to enjoy it at will. Rather than always looking for a ride to the gym, I decided to make it a goal to have my own gym and fun outdoor activities.

Howard's fully-equipped gym at home in Michigan

I have built my environment around my blindness to accommodate my needs and create independence. I am grateful to have the ability to enjoy and share "Howie's Gym," my swimming pool, sand volleyball court, our pond with beachfront, basketball court, horse shoe pit, my running track, and a built-in grill.

One evening while standing around the grill with Chad, having one of our conversations about life, a tiny seed of an idea was planted with my son saying someday we should share our stories from the stage and write a book. A few months would pass and we would bring up this topic again, and each time we both agreed it seemed like a good idea. This tiny seed began to germinate. Months turned into years until finally one day my son said to me, "When is someday?" Chad decided to do something about it. He did not know the "how" but he did make a decision that "when" was *now*.

From the moment I spoke on stage at Ford Auditorium in 1970 in front of 3,000 people, I realized I could open up to an audience in a way that created a connection that was unexpectedly very powerful, and mutually rewarding. How did I get this amazing opportunity?

I was nominated and won the Oscar equivalent of a Salesman Award, based on community involvement and sales volume for the state of Michigan. I was escorted backstage to meet Paul Harvey. We chatted for a few moments. I chuckled to myself and thought, ...*and now the rest of the story!* Paul's famous radio show line. As I walked away, I could not help wondering how I got on stage with the great ABC radio broadcaster Paul Harvey...I had to pinch myself.

I was escorted to the front row with my first wife Kristi and my parents by my side. I was wearing a black tuxedo, looking good and feeling good about my career as an insurance agent. I was introduced and the spotlight picked me up. My wife asked me to stand up. I grabbed her arm as she guided me up to center stage. Are there really 3,000 people out there? How am I going to remember what to say? How did this happen? Full of fear and excitement, I opened my mouth and the words began to flow. When I finished I was in shock with the response from the audience—a standing ovation. Just three years after I lost my sight, I was on top of the business world.

Everyone likes an underdog story and organizations began to see me as someone who could inspire and motivate their employees, especially the sales force. Others saw opportunities for me to inspire young people and I was asked to speak at the National Jaycees Convention. Numerous schools and other organizations contacted me and I felt so honored to have these opportunities.

I started traveling around the United States in the 1970's, sometimes solo. One year I was asked to speak in Omaha, Nebraska, for the Mass Mutual Insurance Company. Traveling independently, I decided to make a stop on my way to the conference and fly into Las Vegas. Perhaps I was remembering my dear friend and mentor, Milt Jo, who had taught me to embrace life, seize the opportunity, and have fun (as described in an earlier chapter).

I remember taking a taxi to my hotel, checking in, and requesting someone to escort me around Vegas during my stay. The hotel manager was called over to speak with me. At first he didn't quite get it, but then I got him to understand that although I was blind, I was there to "see the sights" and have a great time. I also had to make him understand that the kind of "escort" I was looking for was simply someone who knew the strip and was fun to hang out with—someone to guide me to the various casinos and to be my dinner companion. The manager was very helpful, and said he thought I was "remarkable." But it's so simple! Either I could sit around in the dark and feel sorry for myself, or choose to live in the lightness of being alive, engaging with other people, and enjoying life. I never worried about the *how*—the choice is what is critical. In many ways, this *insight I have* is more important than the *sight I don't have.*

After a fun and memorable time in Las Vegas, I went on to Nebraska to join Denny Floden and speak at Mass Mutual. Sales people are not my only audience, by any means. At the request of the former director of Goodwill Industries, I have spoken many times at Goodwill events over the years.

Also, I have spoken to thousands of youth in various schools, sharing my story of how to overcome obstacles and offering children insight into a successful future.

I remember speaking to an elementary school in Swartz Creek, Michigan, and at the end of my talk I hung around as faculty members and a few students came up to chat with me. I felt a firm tug on the bottom of my sport coat as a little girl introduced herself as "Amy." I knelt down to listen more intently. "Thank you for coming today, Mr. Myers," she said. "I didn't know what it was like to be blind until today. Thank you, and I love you." I've never forgotten this brief encounter with a second grader. If my life purpose is being fulfilled, perhaps this is evidence.

In 2009, I was asked to speak for a regional event in Michigan for Farm Bureau Insurance. I told the gentleman who was organizing the event that I wanted my son, Chad, to also speak and to give him a spot on the agenda. Chad had never spoken before at a corporate event but he was primed and full of desire. I experienced a proud moment as I introduced my son to the audience and listened to him explain why most people who set New Year's Resolutions fail, and how to set goals that scare and excite us. He spoke about how my successes personally and professionally were directly related to resilience and persistence. This was the beginning of our father and son speaking career.

Chad decided to get more training in personal development and became a Certified Coach working with LifeSuccess with Bob Proctor, Paul Martinelli, Paul Hutsey (former VP of Prudential Insurance), and Mary Morrissey, the best-selling author who worked with the Dalai Lama, Nelson Mandela and the United Nations. Chad and I began to enjoy a rich collaboration. His training and my life experience led to many discussions on the importance of understanding how our mind controls much of our life, and if we can change our minds, we can change our lives.

We would have three and four-hour conversations about how the unconscious and conscious mind works, and how much of our programming, received in our childhood, is running on auto-pilot, influencing most of the decisions and habits in our adult life. I began to more fully understand myself, and he began to take responsibility for reprogramming his own mind for greater success.

I had found my voice, and my son and I had found how to harmonize. We began sharing my story and his material with several different audiences including my former employer, Mass Mutual. Our dream of speaking together had become a reality. This affirmed just what I heard my son share with our audiences: everything is created twice—first, in the imagination, and finally in the physical realm. Whatever gets manifested into reality was first conceived and seen in the mind's eye. Because of necessity, I've gotten very practiced and good at mind sight and visualization, and cannot recommend it enough for everyone to utilize.

On the way to one of our events in Ohio, Chad decided to look up my former mentor, Denny Floden. He wanted to let him know that we were sharing my success story, since Denny had had a profound and instrumental part in it. We thought that Denny may want to be involved in our personal and professional development organization.

We found that Denny was living in southwest Florida. He was enjoying his "semi-retirement in God's waiting room," he said, and was selling real estate part-time. He immediately said "Yes!" to working with us to reach audiences, and to motivate and inspire people to reach for and achieve big dreams. Over the years some of our clients have been State Farm, Farmers Insurance, Farm Bureau, Mass Mutual, Mary Kay, Michigan Association of Community Mental Health Board, Georgia Nurses Association, Greater Sarasota Realtors Association, Michigan Works, State of Michigan Peer Association, and many veterans' organizations.

Chad Myers, Howard Myers, Denny Floden, Chris Veihl,
keynote presenters at State of Michigan
Community Mental Health Annual Conference (2013)

One of my fondest memories is sharing my story at the Michigan Association of Community Mental Health State Conference as the closing Plenary Speaker. Not only did I speak alongside my son, but also with my mentor Denny Floden, and family friend and psychologist, Chris Veihl. Chad had requested that the conference center set up the stage with a couch, coffee table, plants, and two chairs as we were going to create a consulting room on stage in front of 800 professionals.

The night before we spoke, my son and Chris did a Google search from the hotel lounge for the other plenary speaker, Dr. John Arden. They glanced around the lounge and only two seats away was Dr. Arden. Chris and Chad approached him and shared that we were speaking at the conference and we wanted to meet him. He was delighted and asked us to sit with him. The three of them talked like old friends, connected with common goals and discovered they had a like-minded vision for mental health. They talked about the brain, the future of mental health, and about how we were going to present our material and why. It was almost surreal for me, listening to this fascinating discussion about the "why" of human inner-workings while mapping my own life story, deepening my understanding of my own "Blind Vision," the title of my upcoming speech.

I think Chad and Chris felt especially excited that Dr. Arden was so easy to talk with and that everyone had contributed to the discussion on the same level in their own way. Dr. Arden is a world-class man who has a passion to help the world become more aware and educated on the subject of brain health. What made our connection with Dr. Arden even more interesting was that Denny and I ran into him in the lounge the next evening, the evening before our closing keynote address. We chatted together for some time and collaborated on how we could have the best introduction for "Blind Vision" in front of hundreds of mental health professionals.

The next day, to our great surprise, Dr. Arden walked out on stage along with Chad, Chris, Denny and me when it was time for our presentation. He told the audience that he was humbled to have the opportunity to introduce me and my story. He went on to say that what I had accomplished as a blind man was amazing and impressive. He took a bow in front of me, introduced me to the audience and they all began clapping!

The "Blind Vision" video rolled, sharing a short 10-minute documentary on how I lost my vision in Vietnam, and how I have overcome darkness. Afterwards, the audience honored me with another round of applause. Then we all stood up and asked them to do the same, and to please participate in an exercise with us. Chad requested that everyone close their eyes and not open them until we told them to. The room got completely quiet. It was a very uncomfortable 46 seconds.

We could feel the tension build. We finally said, "Okay, you can now open your eyes." The air came back into the huge auditorium. We shared that each second represented one year of me being blind, as it was the 46th anniversary of the loss of my eyesight in Vietnam. With the audience now even more engaged, we began the "live consultation" part of our presentation, where Chad interviewed

Denny and me in our onstage "living room" and Chris gave his insights as a psychologist.

In brief, Blind Vision is about how I transformed my life from a victim of circumstances to taking ownership and responsibility for my so-called disability. Our presentation covers the importance of purpose, self-discipline, and most importantly, how building a connection with someone who believes in you can change your life.

For my story to have the most impact on audiences, we knew it needed to be relatable and also give people some concepts that were like concrete steps to stand on. We outlined the entire story around four basic principles named and developed by Chad. He shared that these came to him in the wee hours of the morning one day, the ideas crystallizing in his mind as he sat down to "download" as the ideas poured in and through him. It was a few months before our presentation and we had been talking about it nearly every day. Chad called me and I can't remember him ever having more excitement in his voice. He told me that he had woken up earlier with the word "CARE" across the screen of his mind. He snapped up a pencil and immediately started writing down C. A. R. E. He told me his pencil seemed to be guided by another force and he wrote pages and pages. Once he was done, the rough draft and outline for the presentation was right in front of him. The way for me to use my story to help others is all about CARE. This is the heart of the matter: Connection, Aspiration, Rewiring and Empowering. Chad gives brief descriptions of each here:

CONNECTION. All great coaches, therapists, teachers, parents and leaders know that before we can empower others we have to build a connection. Connecting takes courage because it requires vulnerability to honor one's journey without judgment. It takes belief in another's worth to begin the process of change and growth.

ASPIRATION. To aspire means to breathe, to eagerly desire, to rise up and soar. To become a great leader, parent, coach, manager, or mentor requires imagination and creativity but these qualities can be inhibited by an unhealthy mindset. Negativity chokes us.

REWIRING. I spent a great deal of time researching everything I could get my hands on regarding motivation and personal development, neuro-psychology, and the power of relationships. Growing up, I had wondered why my dad had become so over-the-top successful even though he was blind. As an adult with my masters in education, certification as a life coach and years of experiences as an educator, I was able to not just wonder about the reasons for my dad's success, I was determined to understand them thoroughly. In partnership with Chris Veihl, a licensed therapist with a Masters in Counseling, we began to unravel and analyze Howard's story.

We wanted to understand exactly how Howard was able to go from the depths of depression to a heightened sense of confidence and self-awareness. Simply put, we concluded that he had "rewired" his brain, or as some might say, reprogrammed his mind. This reprogramming had taken place through repetition and focused attention; the reprogramming developed new neuron-pathways. Today we are aware of self-directed neuroplasticity, our minds' ability to change our brain. For my dad, it was a matter of survival. Chris, my dad and I were committed to this inquiry: If a blind guy can rewire his brain for survival in a sighted world, is there any reason one can't rewire for success in the same world?

EMPOWERING. When we truly connect with people, aspire for something better and rewire our brains for success, we are able to focus on our abilities instead of our limitations. We gain power from having a positive vision, and we begin to live a life of gratitude where we give hope and help to others. When we are empowered, we can empower others to succeed.

When my father and I speak to audiences, we find that using these four distinctions helps to communicate our message of hope. We live for the opportunity to help people release themselves from the chokehold of negativity, do what it takes to rewire their mind, and create a bright and optimistic life just as Howard has demonstrated so powerfully.

***

The four of us—Denny, Chris, Chad and I—all stood up in front of the audience. Denny began by saying, "I had a coach who believed in me before I believed in myself." I noticed his voice quiver and wondered if he was displaying emotion in front of all these people.

Denny elbowed me and I took the cue to continue his sentiment. I said with tears in my eyes, "Denny was asked to pay it forward and he believed in me until I could believe in myself!"

I passed on the nudge to my son. "Today I would like to leave you with this," I heard Chad say. "Please believe in your clients until they can believe in themselves!" The audience all stood up and gave us a standing ovation. It was an amazing feeling and something I will never forget.

At the conclusion of our seminar, several people came forward with tears, handshakes, and hugs. Dr. Arden hugged me and my son saying this was an extremely inspirational story and to please continue our campaign. Later I learned he had tears in his eyes. Mark Lowis, the man responsible for booking us at that event, shared the same feelings with a big hug. People began to surround us and share how much they appreciated our story.

Suddenly I felt my hand being gripped tightly as I heard a lady crying. In a moment, she stopped crying enough to speak to me. She told me that part of my speech had meant a lot to her personally, the part about a man, Joe Schomsky, my former boss, who had influenced me in so many positive ways. "Thank you, Howard," she said. "You honored my grandfather today. He passed away several years ago, and to hear all of the beautiful things you shared about him made me realize how important life is!"

Life can be quite interesting; forty-five years earlier, Joe Shomsky had given me a chance in life and I was able to share it with his granddaughter in the audience all these years later. I simply shook my head in disbelief of the chance of her being in the audience that day.

"Mountaintops are for views and inspiration,
but fruit is grown in the valleys."

—*Rev. Billy Graham (1918-2018)*

Chapter 12
You Have A Choice

Shifting *from trauma to triumph* is a process. It is not possible to make this shift until one understands the metaphor written in the following poem:

"I walk down the street.
There is a deep hole in the sidewalk.
I fall in.
I am lost... I am helpless.
It isn't my fault.
It takes forever to find a way out.

"I walk down the same street.
There is a deep hole in the sidewalk.
I pretend I don't see it.
I fall in again.
I can't believe I am in the same place.
But, it isn't my fault.
It still takes me a long time to get out.

"I walk down the same street.
There is a deep hole in the sidewalk.
I see it is there.
I still fall in. It's a habit.
My eyes are open.
I know where I am.
It is my fault. I get out immediately.

"I walk down the same street.
There is a deep hole in the sidewalk.
I walk around it.

"I walk down another street."

— Portia Nelson,

"There's a Hole in My Sidewalk:
The Romance of Self-Discovery"

What are you focusing on? The holes or the new road? Darkness or light? I choose to live in the light. What are you *choosing* to focus on? Is it darkness or light? The light stems from my FOCUS on what I can do and let go of what I cannot do. In essence, what my blindness has taught me is to control the controllable and let the rest go. In reality, the only thing I can control is how I choose to respond to life.

Blind Vision has taught me to have a bigger vision of life. I live in my mind now. I cannot afford to focus on blindness, sameness, and darkness. It will suck my soul dry. I have to CHOOSE to live in the light by using my imagination and visualizing what I want in my life. I believe this is what is meant to walk by faith and not by sight. You have a choice. I do not. We know that 80% of life is perceived through our eyes. Since I do not have visual input, I now must use my own mind and imagination to create my reality. Maybe I have an advantage over you...I feel had no option but to make the choice to live in the light.

Many of you may be familiar with the Prayer of Saint Francis. I believe this prayer has changed my life for the better, and I say it often:

"Lord, allow me, Howard Myers, to be an instrument of your peace. Where there is hatred, let me sow love..."

By focusing on compassion and letting go of judgment of myself and others, I am sowing love.

"Where there is darkness, light…"

I go to bed in darkness and wake up in darkness, but I choose to live in the light. This is what living in the light means to me: I choose an attitude of gratitude. I ask whom may I show an act of kindness to. I choose to look for the good in all things and all people, starting with myself.

"Where there is doubt, faith."

Doubt is an emotion, faith is a decision. Decision is the key to change.

"Where there is injury, pardon."

I learned a long time ago, it is not what people do to you, it is how you choose to respond to what they do to you. At the end of the day, it is between you and your Creator.

"Where there is sadness, joy."

Embrace the sadness and over time you will experience the joy. Joy starts with gratitude, my saving grace. I focus on what I do have and not on what I cannot have.

This prayer has changed my life by reminding me that I can have everything I want in life with the right attitude and the right belief system. It has been my desire that by sharing my story with you, it will inspire you to create your own blind vision and a new reality.

We are all writing our own story called life. We can write a new narrative by connecting with someone who cares, who will challenge and inspire us to move through the difficulties in life (even the trauma). You can move toward triumph and empower yourself to rewrite your story.

If you would like to go deeper into the principles of change that I have used on my journey to triumph, I invite you to contact us:

<u>www.BlindVisionAssociates.com</u>

LIVE IN THE LIGHT.

"If you want others to be happy, practice compassion. If you want to be happy, practice compassion."

—Dalai Lama

Chapter 13
Blind Vision: The Ripple Effect

Mended Souls

My relationship with Howard Myers began in 2010 when, through mutual acquaintances, I was introduced to his son, Chad. He and I discussed doing some consulting work together and he shared his father's story with me. I was instantly blown away by Howard's accomplishments and knew I had to get to know him better.

We eventually met and he shared his story of being blinded in Vietnam, his struggles following that tragedy, and some of his life accomplishments since that fateful day in 1967. He shared many stories with me, but he told me one thing that has forever changed my own life and subsequently the lives of many others. "Chris," Howard said, "I go to sleep every night in the dark and I wake up every day to the same darkness, yet I make a conscious decision to live in the light every day of my life. I choose to focus my attention on what I CAN do and not what I am not able to do."

Shortly after that meeting, the Mindworks Performance Group was formed and I have been privileged and honored to share the stage with Howard and Chad and Denny Floden, as we have shared Howard's story and the C.A.R.E principles of personal growth to many different audiences.

Perhaps the greatest contribution that I have received from Howard is that I have shared his daily practice of "choosing to live in the light" with hundreds of young children and adolescents that I have the privilege of working with each day. One of my roles in life is that I am the Clinical Director of a residential treatment center that provides treatment to young people who have been removed from their homes due to extreme neglect and abuse. These children have lived many "dark nights" and for many of them their immediate futures are greatly in doubt. Through Howard's story and continued willingness to share, many of these children understand what it means to" chose to live in the light" and their resilience and inner strength has grown. Howard's legacy of resilience and inner strength will live on through many lives; many fractured souls have been mended by this man's inner courage and willingness to persevere and love.

Chris Veihl

Clinical Director. Family Therapist. Speaker. Trainer

Insight vs. Sight

At the age of 15, I met Howard Myers. We heard a blind man had moved into to the neighborhood and soon after discovered his blindness was caused by an explosion in Vietnam.

My older brother had gone to Vietnam and came back a changed person, though not with visible wounds such as Howard and so many others had sustained. He had gotten married and moved on with his life. Howard became that older brother figure in my life.

I was playing high school football and working out to stay in shape. Howard has always been an active man and we became running partners. We ran around the neighborhood and went to the gym to work out.

He offered me a job to drive him to his insurance appointments. I was able to get off school early, for work release, to go drive Howard. At 16, driving a car for a living was my dream job. Little did I know the impact on my life that dream job would have.

At first I would just drive him to his appointments or to the office; I didn't pay much attention to what was going on. I soon realized

I was going places and seeing thing others my age didn't have the opportunity to do. I started to pay attention. I dressed a little better when I picked him up—slacks instead of jeans, button down shirt instead of a pullover. I will never forget the day Howard called and wanted me to pick him up at the office and I thought we were going to go to the gym to work out, so I showed up in shorts and a tee-shirt. Howard was in a suit and tie. I walked in as he was coming out of Joe Shomsky's office where he had been trying to convince Joe to sponsor me as a life insurance agent when I turned 18. The look on Joe's face when he saw me in the office in that outfit confirmed his decision not to sponsor me as an agent. We got to the car and Howard told me what he was doing in Joe's office and asked me not to wear that outfit to the office again, and said, "I bet the look on Joe's face was priceless."

One of the things I will never forget from those days is the way Howard interacted with his clients, carefully listening to their needs. Also, it was clear that he placed a high value on his family and spending time with them. And I remember that he would always ask questions about everyday things that I took for granted. In the spring, he would ask about the farming activities—what was being planted, the number of tractors in the fields, and so forth. Summer's inquires would be, "…describe what the clouds look like. Are they the big, white puffy ones? Or are they dark and grey?" He always noticed when the smell of rain was in the air. In the fall, he would ask me to describe the different autumn colors of the leaves changing.

After high school graduation, I moved away, went to school and became a registered nurse. I've never told Howard this, but I would often call him after a bad day at work. It was challenging, to say the least, taking care of a 3-year-old burn victim or an 11-year-old that was terminally abused by his father. I needed someone to talk to that had faced adversity but kept his faith.

We would talk about things going on in our lives, family, jobs, or recent trips. I didn't talk about the details of my emotional state, but he knew the look on my face just from hearing my voice. Howard's insight is extraordinary. He would always say an encouraging word or just remind me to keep my faith in God.

The things I learned in those early days still serve me today:

- Always have time for my family, keep my faith.
- As a nurse, I need to pay attention to the little details.
- Listen and be of service to others. As of this writing, I am the President of the Georgia Nurses Association, an organization representing over 150,000 licensed nurses in the state of Georgia.
- Most importantly; it is better to show up to an event overdressed than underdressed.

Howard, thank you for your life-long friendship.

Richard Lamphier

President, Georgia Nurses Association

The Heart Finds a Way

One person stands out in my heart and mind above all in the Crim Festival of Races, Howard Myers. Howard called me in 1982 and said he was blind and he wanted to run the Crim. He had it clearly worked out in his mind! He would run tethered to the wrist of Bobby Crim who could direct him verbally about any problems – such as curbs, any litter (runners often pitched water bottles away as they run). Man, I was at a loss of words for this one. Bobby was a competitive runner who wanted to register a strong time in the Crim. Howard, a soft-spoken speaker was determined he could run with several thousand other runners. It was not even possible to convince this Vietnam veteran that at least, this might not be possible. And to secure it, he had anchored a business man who donated a couple of thousand dollars in pledges. Mark Bauman and John Gault pledged that they would help train Howard.

Convinced I may never direct this race again (which had stolen my heart long ago), I approached Bobby. He was interested. He met Howard and said OK. It was the beginning of a new friendship between the two which has lasted all these years. And Howard became my dearest friend, too. He taught me a strong lesson: "If your heart wants to do something, you will find the way".

By participating in the Crim, Howard has raised thousands and thousands of dollars for mentally-challenged athletes. He has enticed thousand of runners with his will "to just do it," and he inspires and awes thousands of spectators who have watched him race the Crim. With his courage and strong dedication to Special Olympians, he brings hope, pride and dedication to the Crim. He is more than "special," he is inspirational, and everyone who has ever raced the Crim knows Howard Myers. Anyone would say, "Howard is the *what* and *why* of the Crim."

He is the inspiration of thousands of runners who have never had that "special moment" of conversing with a man so "special," but who have watched him cross that finish line of life over and over again with big smile on his face—the smile of freedom, of triumph over tragedy, of knowing your efforts make a real difference.

You cannot stand on the Crim finish line and see this man tethered to Bobby's wrist and not understand the *why* of the Crim. You are overjoyed with the possibilities of life and the strength and courage of this Vietnam vet, blinded by a landmine, who learned to tackle life and *live* it to its fullest. That's Howard Myers. He represents the courage of all the athletes of Special Olympics, and of everyone who meets a huge challenge with heart, courage, and determination.

Lois Craig

17-year director of the Crim Road Race

<u>No Time for Excuses</u>

I first met Howard Myers over the phone, and from that first conversation I knew he was a great guy, full of optimism, with a contagious positive attitude about life. What I did not know is that he had no eyesight. It was never mentioned; it is just not how Howard Myers defines himself.

I had answered an incoming call at the brokerage firm I had just started working for, and it was Howard. There was an instant connection between him and me. I had no idea that Howard was blind when I initially took that call years ago, and it was somewhat shocking to me when I found out the truth from a fellow employee when the call had ended. Howard's optimism (something I also cling to in my own life) and excitement to simply be alive and well that day was somewhat perplexing, but nothing short of inspirational to me.

The fact that he did not mention his downfall and did not feel the need to—even using language like "I watched the game the other day," or "Did you see the game this weekend?," implying he could very well see with his own eyes—was again somewhat perplexing but fascinating to me. Simply put, he did not dwell on the negatives that had happened to him because—*why would you? Who has time for that?* It instantly put my life in perspective for me, something that continues to this day. What Howard did not know upon our first conversation was that I had suddenly and somewhat tragically lost my father on Christmas day about one year prior to our conversation. It was something I was still struggling with daily.

Over the next two years or so, Howard and I spoke weekly if not daily, often times about insurance work but often about life's trials and tribulations as well, developing a deeper connection in the process.

Howard is more or less a mentor to so many. I had the pleasure one day to make it out to his home and finally put a face to a name and shake the man's hand who had taught me more than he could imagine in a very short amount of time, despite feeling as if we had known each other forever.

Howard's jubilant and sometimes harsh-reality stories and attitude played a significant role in my own grieving process (from losing my father). Our conversations helped my mental stability, and helped me get my work life and my personal life back on track—something I am eternally grateful for.

There are countless, specific conversations I could share, but to sum it up…Howard Myers and the way he approaches every single day, with no desire for pity and no time for excuses, helped mold me into a better person and into the man I am today.

Occasionally I wonder if my father had anything to do with putting Howard and me in touch. I know my father, a very similar man to Howard in many regards, would appreciate the time he has given me, what he has taught me, and what he has done for me without even knowing it.

For now, I'll chalk up my fortuitous connection with Howard to luck, timing, whatever…and continue to be thankful for the mere opportunity to know and learn from this man. What he shares is invaluable to ALL of us, if we simply take the time to listen.

John Anton Vogl II

Business Development Advisor. Entry Point Advisor Network

Knowing What to Focus On

I've worked with Howard Myers since the summer of 2013. Howard needed help with a Medicare product for a friend of his and he reached out to a BCBS affiliate. The BCBS affiliate gave me a call and asked if I'd be willing to assist them. I met with Howard and his friend and guided them in the right direction. This direction did not result in a sale for me, however, based on my professional recommendation, Howard's friend was able to get the right policy for his needs directly from the insurance carrier… and at a much lower cost than any product I had to offer. At that moment, Howard realized that I handle my business the same way he does. We don't do what is best for ourselves; we focus on the customer's need and do what's best for them.

Because of this shared philosophy, we formed a working relationship where I assisted Howard with his clients that had health insurance questions (mainly due to the Affordable Care Act). This working relationship then transformed into a wonderful friendship that I am truly grateful for.

Spending time with Howard the last few years has helped me grow in many ways—both professionally and personally. We have been able to help so many people with their health insurance decisions that my book of business has more than doubled—all while focusing on what is best for the customer. Howard's influence has helped me grow my business more than I could have imagined and put me in a position to become a partner in my agency (which I did in 2015).

In working so closely with Howard through hundreds of cases, we got to know each other on a very personal level. He has been a true mentor to me. His can-do attitude and his positive perspective on dealing with the many challenges of life have a tremendous effect on all those who surround him. I am truly blessed to be able to call Howard Myers my friend.

Micah Widder

President, Security First Benefits

Lucky to be Alive

I have known Howard since North Branch High School. He was a jock, I was a rebel. Even though we were quite different, we became friends and fortunately for me, the friendship continued beyond graduation.

A male graduating in the early 60s knew his fate. You got a job (they were plentiful at the time), saved up for a new car, and waited for your letter from the draft board. There were ways of avoiding the draft, but most just accepted it as the "dues" you pay to be in America. Howard was one of these. I had a deferment because I was in an apprenticeship, which was like kicking the can down the road, knowing I would get mine when I became a journeyman.

I was able to visit Howard and other high school buddies when they were finishing up boot camp at Fort Knox. Not long afterward, I visited him again, but this time at a VA Hospital in Pennsylvania. I felt I was the same young man, but Howard was different. He was angry at first, but eventually accepted his fate.

My next visit was at the Hines Rehabilitation Hospital in Chicago. I watched Howard learning how to get around in the facility, outside on the streets, and even in downtown Chicago without assistance. I had the privilege knowing he received a Purple Heart, a decoration of honor he will never see.

As the years passed, I was always amazed with what Howard could do, and by his positive attitude. Several times we went boating and one day, after some "liquid courage," another friend and I convinced Howard he could water ski—to our amazement, he did! He even dropped his ski like he had done in high school and slalomed around the lake like a sighted man!

Sharing these times with Howard gave me a mindset that if you believe in yourself, you can do the unexpected. After a recent tragic car accident, I had to buy into everything I had "gleaned" from being a friend of Howard.

#1. You are lucky to be alive

#2. Don't feel sorry for yourself

#3. Mindset, believe in yourself

Howard is my mentor, his wisdom my answer to adversity. Being his friend has allowed me to become a stronger and better person. Thanks to Howard, my glass is always half full.

Walt Severn

Let's Pray About This

Howard Myers is one of the most amazing, inspirational people I know. It is truly a privilege to know him, and even greater honor to call him my friend. I am so thankful for his service to our country. Howard served in a time when it was not popular to be a US soldier, in a time where a multitude of Americans did not appreciate his sacrifice. He did not let their cloud of ungraciousness dampen his spirit. And, he refused to let his disability define him.

I came to know Howard 20 years ago when I worked for my father's business, as he was the agent that handled the company's health insurance. Through the years of working together, I became more than a client; I became friends with him and his wife, Debbie. Howard would call quite often to make sure that everything was going well with the policy, my job, and my family.

Our relationship has continued to grow. "Let's pray about this," Howard will say to me on the phone...just when it is the perfect thing to say. We share prayer requests and encourage one another to trust in God.

Howard has faced many arduous obstacles since that fateful day in 1967, and he knows that there are still more ahead. He will continue to be an overcomer, trusting God, just as he always has, to carry him through.

Sherry Gleason

Courage

I've known Howard for most of my 40-year career as a Brokerage General Agent. He has been great to work with but most of all, he has been inspirational. Trying to comprehend what Howard has gone through and how he has handled it is the hardest, as most of us would not have had the inner fortitude to do so. From his rude awakening in the hospital to find out he will be blind for the rest of his life, this remarkable man decided the best plan was to make the most out of what was handed him. And that is what he did. I consider him to be a true friend and a great example of one who is the epitome of courage.

Daniel W. Wonnell, CLU, ChFC

Highlight of the Conference

It's clear! Howard, you were the highlight of our conference. I am so excited about how this went and I want to thank you and your team, especially you, Howard, for the generous spirit of sharing

Blind Vision that allowed us to have you at the MACMHB Annual Spring Conference AND the Michigan Department of Community Health Cross-Cutting and Integrated Practices Conference.

Mark Lowis

National Trainer, Professor, State of Michigan Community Mental Health

Immeasurable Worth

I have to say that the training I have received from Chad and Howard Myers is the most important training I have received in the 14 years I have been an agent. I cannot articulate its value in brief. Its benefits are too comprehensive and numerous for that. Each week, I've singled out one idea that is of immeasurable worth.

John Kaminski Mass Mutual Financial Group

BSME, MBA, CLU, ChFC, CASL

Unique, Personal and Relevant

I recently had the opportunity to hear Howard Myers. I was truly inspired by his message and the tremendous attitude he brought to one of our regional kick offs! His story is unique, personal and relevant to our industry.

Vic Verchereau, LUTCF, LLIF
Vice President Marketing, Farm Bureau Insurance

Attitude Determines Your Altitude—And My Dad SOARS!

My father, Howard Myers, has lived life as an extraordinary example of determination and resiliency. He has impacted my life at the core, teaching by example that the only disability in life is a bad attitude.

That's a tall order some days as I face the immense challenges of parenting an autistic child. My dad has taught me to never, ever quit, and be relentless in your pursuit. From him, I have learned to trust in the dark, see with the eyes of your heart, believe in the good in all people and all things, and dwell in the light.

His legacy of friendships, the countless connections he's made over the years, the admiration and respect and joy he brings to others, reminding them not to take their sight or their life for granted, have shaped who I am today. He "walks the talk" as he lives consistent with what he loves to teach: Gratitude is Kin; whatever you focus on you will get more of; and that we are too blessed to be stressed.

A girl could only dream of having a father like mine. I am blessed beyond measure to stand on his shoulders to see the world as I've been privileged to see. His faithfulness to God, his wife, his family and friends has provided an unshakable foundation for his children to explore the world, strive for our dreams, become our highest self and serve others.

His altruism has been contagious, inspiring me to embrace my son's autism diagnosis with courage. Courage can be fear that has said its prayers as it was a shocking new journey I had to embark on. Desiring to "be the change I wanted to see in the world," I set out to provide more autism support services for my county and opened an autism center, a huge possibility and commitment I stepped into.

My dad's wisdom empowers me in all of my endeavors, big and small: Be the captain of your thoughts, not the captive; you're beautiful inside if you have a beautiful heart; live above my circumstances; focus on blessings not troubles; if you can believe it, you can achieve it; always go the extra mile, and as he always does, lead by example. He taught me to love, love more, forgive, forgive more, move forward, and always strive to be the best version of myself. He believes one should never stop improving, live inspired, and be the change you wish to see in the world. He taught me to win mental warfare, how to discipline your thoughts, choosing them like you would your wardrobe. My dad likes to say to keep your chin up, and keep smiling because you're prettier with a smile.

The world is a better place because of my daddy, my war hero, and my best friend. I am proud beyond words in print that my heart can see better because of the vision of this man. I remember that my attitude is what matters—life is only 10% circumstances, 90% attitude—and attitude determines your altitude.

Thanks dad for working out in the dark to become a better man when you could've felt sorry for yourself. Thanks dad for showing others reminding us that determination, grit, courage, tenacity, resilience and commitment to family never go out of style. You're a timeless man impacting now and eternity.

Love your forever daughter, Jennifer Myers

Live in the Light

What's my excuse? I asked myself. I met Howard a few years ago for the first time when my fiancée Chad introduced us. I was already inspired when I watched his video of running alone while blind. I ran in the past, but for various reasons stopped. It seemed I always had a "good excuse." After seeing Howard do what it takes to run, even though completely blind, I was determined to run again and I did. He has taught me that my health is my greatest wealth and that we can overcome any adversity with the right attitude. It is truly inspirational that he can maintain a positive attitude and live in the light, even while in darkness.

Joanna Wnuk

Thanks for the Mentoring

Howard has been somewhat generous in calling me his mentor and I take great pride in having been a part of his life and in helping him become such a success. As the Assistant General Agent for Mass Mutual, it was my job to recruit and train new agents. Therefore, in many respects, I was just doing my job.

When I hired him, it quickly became evident to me that I had no idea how to best guide, teach, train, or mentor a blind person. Before total panic set in, Howard saved the day by telling me,

"I don't want to be treated like a disabled blind guy. Treat me as you would any other recruit." So I did—partly to honor his request and partly because I didn't have a clue how else to do it. *Thanks for helping me out, Howard.*

Having competed at a highest level on national championship teams while at the University of Michigan, I felt I understood the concepts of setting goals, hard work, and the determination necessary to succeed. Howard provided me with a whole new dimension and understanding of these terms, however. *Thanks, Howard.*

By example, he also helped me grow and overcome some hang-ups regarding my own unhappy childhood. I heard a saying: "I cried and cried because I had no shoes, until I met a man who had no feet." Watching Howard overcome his obstacles made my childhood obstacles seem rather small in comparison. *Thanks, Howard. I needed to learn that.*

His grit and determination was inspiring. I should also thank Howard for eliminating a lot of time spent listening to excuses from other agents for non-performance. It was difficult for other agents to come up with an excuse that had merit when the blind guy is succeeding and they were not—so often, they just didn't try.

Many people are uncomfortable around those with disabilities. Howard's sense of humor is flat out charming and puts people at ease. One day he was in another agent's office on the ground floor that looked out over the parking lot and he called up to my office, telling me to hurry down. I ran downstairs and he told me to check out the pretty blonde in the red convertible. When I asked how he knew the car was red, he snorted, "I'm just blind, not color blind!"

On occasion, I went to his office and stated that it was dark and I couldn't see because the lights were off. "I hadn't noticed," he responded and told me to turn them on. "Are they on?" he asked. When I told him they were, he said, "Damn. The lights never work for me—it's still dark." *Thanks for the laughs, Howard. And thanks for saving the agency money on our utility bills.*

He also showed me how to better connect with my customers by listening and getting them involved in the process. I would show up with a beautifully prepared multi-page presentation and wonder why the customer didn't buy what I knew was the best solution for him. Howard would show up with a pen, yellow legal pad and a rate book and guide the customer into writing down their needs, wants, and desires. When the amount of insurance needed was determined, the customer looked up the rate, calculated the premium and usually bought something. *Thanks for teaching me how to better listen to and involve the customer, Howard.*

Thanks for the privilege of being your mentor and friend, Howard. I hope you learned as much from me as I did from you. Not only have you been a great friend in my life, by being who you are made you my mentor as well.

Denny Floden

Captain Phogg Enterprises, 7-time Hot Air Balloon World Champion

*Chris, Chad, Howard and Denny meet
to work on Blind Vision book (2017)*

"Howard essentially rewired his brain to maximize new skills to become a highly effective person."

—*John Arden, Ph.D.*

Chapter 14
The Brain Science Behind Howard's Journey

By Dr. John Arden, Neuropsychologist

Everyone loves the archetypal hero, a person who against all odds saves a village, or rescues a family from peril at risk of losing his life. People who have accomplished such heroic feats are rare indeed. But they are not the only people who have heroic acts. A person who transforms personal tragedy into triumph and then inspires others who have suffered great loss, that person too is heroic. I have just described Howard Myers. Howard and his son, Chad, share how he transformed personal catastrophe into triumph in this inspiring book.

I met Howard a few years ago and was immediately in awe of his heroic story. We were both giving keynotes at a conference in Michigan and his son Chad asked me to introduce his dad. I said, "You have immense pride in your dad, and for good reason!" He said that he and his dad wanted me to speak about the psychology and neuroscience of his success. It is a great honor to be asked to write my thoughts about this book of triumph over extreme adversity. It serves as inspiration to anyone who has suffered a great loss and then wonders, "Should I just give up?" He details how, by not giving up, he gained a life that far exceeded everyone's expectations.

What is resiliency? What is bouncing back after trauma? When you are dealt a catastrophe, how would you not only survive but **thrive**? Unfortunately, far too many people who encounter tragedy give up. They don't fight back and rise to the challenge like Howard. He did not let blindness defeat his vision of transcendence over catastrophe. He had in "sight" the person he wanted to be, and perhaps saw beyond his own expectations.

I am reminded of how Ludwig Beethoven transcended deafness to transform Western music for all time. He went through a period of despair and self-doubt. He wondered if he could endure and suffer deafness—of all impairments!—just as, according to many, he was becoming the "new Mozart." When he found out that there was no cure for his deafness, he wrote a suicide note to his brothers. But instead of giving up, Beethoven wrote the Third Symphony, known as "Eroica," for its historic and revolutionary role in shifting music to a new era. The Eroica is considered one of the five greatest pieces of music ever written; two of the remaining four were composed by Beethoven when he was completely deaf!

Beethoven's symphonies excite the prefrontal cortex and we could speculate that he supercharged his prefrontal cortex to write them. Had he simply written pleasant melodies we would not know him as the colossal figure that he came to be. So what is the prefrontal cortex? It is the most advanced part of the brain. The last to evolve, the CEO of the brain, we can call it the brain's brain. Without a healthy prefrontal cortex (especially the left prefrontal cortex), you would sit back and let others do everything for you and you would never be satisfied.

Howard expressed a "can do" attitude while orchestrating a relentless effort that combined with the careful attentiveness necessary to adjust to unforeseen obstacles and details. That is quite a feat for a mature prefrontal cortex. But from a developmental perspective, he incurred the catastrophic injury at age 19 when his prefrontal cortex was not fully developed. Men and women do not fully develop their prefrontal cortex until their mid-twenties or later! This means that Howard was putting demands upon a part of the brain that was not yet mature.

He was pushing his prefrontal cortex to develop in ways that demanded that he juggle immensely complicated details to succeed despite seemingly insurmountable barriers. As he developed his prefrontal cortex, its abilities with goal-directed behavior, decision-making, and frustration tolerance exceeded many other adolescents who were on cruise control. The bottom line was that Howard was dealt this horrific injury at a time that the part of his brain that would have helped him control his anger and grief was developing. But he managed to master the challenges while his prefrontal cortex was going through its last growth spurt in such a way to make him amazingly tenacious, skilled, and talented at managing his emotions.

Another brain-based aspect to consider in how Howard was so successful is this: there is a big difference between approach and avoidance/withdrawal behavior. He approached life when he was down, but never down for the count. Approach-behaviors activate the left hemisphere and are associated with positive emotions. In contrast, over-activation of the right hemisphere is associated with anxiety and depression. In other words, by putting one foot in front of the other and approaching success, even when the obstacles seemed overwhelming, he was able to keep his mood up and keep himself from falling into a pool of overwhelming despair and depression.

For people who think that the challenges are too great and success does not seem possible, consider the adage from Alcoholics Anonymous, "Fake it until you make it." Put another way: keep trying to do what you have not yet accomplished until you are able to do it. Think of how hard it is to learn a new language. In the beginning, the language sounds completely foreign and you cannot replicate even its most basic sounds. But through the power of neuroplasticity, you build circuits in your brain to make those sounds and recall the new vocabulary. As you develop the capacity to carry on an actual conversation, you grow a wide network of neuronal connections in your brain. This is what is meant by the phrase, "cells that fire together wire together." You practice the skills you want to develop and those skills, over time, come to you more easily. Howard essentially rewired his brain to maximize new skills to become a highly effective person.

Two psychologists found that three factors were common to highly successful, stress-hardy people. Termed the "three C's," these factors are commitment, control, and challenge. Together they represent the characteristics of people who can deal with stress in stride, and turn extremely demanding situations into success.

The first is "commitment," which represents motivation to act according to your values. Howard did not want to be dependent upon others. He was committed to contribute to his friends, family, and co-workers as well as to you, the reader, by sharing the wisdom contained in this book. The second factor is "control," which represents a realistic measure of what is possible. In the spirit of Reinhold Niebuhr's "Serenity Prayer," he had a vision of what he could do and did not waste his energy on what he could not do. Instead of "setting his sights" on being an airline pilot, he chose a profession that he knew he could master, despite others' lack of confidence in his efforts.

The third factor is "challenge." Perhaps because some people did not think that he could do it, Howard took up the challenge of showing them and himself that he could become an insurance agent and a role model for others with disabilities. Howard's success is, in part, because he demonstrated how the three C's work together. When he was told that he would not be able to succeed as an insurance agent or even pass the tests, he made a commitment to himself that he would do everything he could to be successful. He managed to control the factors of preparation, constantly adjusting to the demands. And when told he could not succeed —don't bother trying— he took that as an invitation to rise to the challenge.

Chapter 14: The Brain Science Behind Howard's Journey

Howard did not transcend tragedy in isolation from others. He thrived through the support from other people who believe in him. Howard used that support, his *connections*, by working with them to calibrate his efforts to best fit his changing needs. Instead of passively receiving support, he shaped it so that he maximized the chance for success.

Howard's attitude kept him focused on success. Had he been a pessimist his life would have been quite different. How would you answer this question: "Is the glass full or completely empty?" This extreme version of the question about pessimism versus optimism is timeless. Do you see possibilities or nothing but insurmountable limitations? The attitudinal differences between optimism and pessimism predict success or failure as well as life satisfaction or never being satisfied. Hopefulness is leaning forward while helplessness is leaning backward and dragging your feet as people try to help you out. Howard leaned forward and made something great of his life. Things would have been so different had he not entertained hope.

It would have been so easy to sit back and take disability payments, to live out his life being dependent on the system. But that was not good enough for Howard. He would not have respected himself. Even now, he could simply retire and enjoy his retirement. Yet, he wants to share his *blind vision* to help others who feel like giving up. He wants and needs to be a contributor. This book of inspiration is part of the contribution.

Howard's inspiring story of resiliency, courage, and tenacity is for everyone. However overwhelming your challenge, your loss, and its duration, giving up should not be an option. He has shown that people can, through the belief in a realistic optimistic future with meaning, promote their own posttraumatic-growth. The potential for positive growth, post-trauma, has been exemplified by reports that up to one-half of trauma victims describe some sort of positive outcome post-trauma.

Blind Vision

Howard's posttraumatic growth involved discarding hopelessness and embracing realistic optimism about his life. Hope promotes control and a realistic sense of strength. The changes to his relationships allowed him to deepen intimacy and share feelings about what happened as well as aspirations for the future. His new sense of self was wiser and he became a more compassionate person.

Like others who experience posttraumatic growth, Howard supports those who face challenges by telling his inspirational story in his book. The importance of developing meaning posttrauma was also described in the book, *Man's Search for Meaning*, by Victor Frankl. Despite enduring the horrors of the Auschwitz concentration camp, Frankl embraced a transcendent sense of meaning, demonstrating that deeply traumatized people can move on to wisdom and growth. In fact, many people who have been horribly traumatized have gone on to gain a deep sense of meaning and satisfaction with life. In this book, Howard offers personal evidence of how you or someone you love can transcend challenges and develop greater meaning and satisfaction in life.

ACKNOWLEDGMENTS

People come into our life for a reason, a season, or a lifetime. Fortunately for me, I have had great mentors and many wonderful friends that have come into my life for various reasons along the way to help me to be where I am today. *Blind Vision* has truly been a team effort. Without the combined efforts of all those involved, my message would not reach the people I most want to touch.

I deeply appreciate the contributions of Chris Veihl. Eight years ago, my son Chad met Chris at a local gym. Chris invited Chad over for dinner and the two of them soon knew why so many people had told them they needed to meet. Chris and Chad have been like brothers over the years, and in essence, Chris has been like another son to me. He is the Clinical Director of Crossroads for Youth, a trauma expert, an incredible human-being, and one of the best family therapists I have ever met. His calm, emphatic attitude towards life and my family has been a godsend. Once Chris heard of our *Blind Vision* project he took great interest in my story. Chris and Chad began meeting on a regular basis, having deep, long discussions as only a life coach and therapist could. Often times I had no idea what they were talking about but over the years I slowly began to understand what these two intelligent, emotionally-grounded men wanted to share with the world through my story.

Chris Veihl spent countless hours in the war room during this book writing project, offering his knowledge and giving careful insight from a therapist's point of view. I lived the story, Chris and Chad helped tell it.

I want to thank and honor my wife, Debbie, for her loyalty to me and to my dream of sharing my story to help as many people as possible, which we knew meant somehow getting it published as a book. I appreciate her giving me rides to Chris's office, putting up with the long nights, weekends, and countless hours she had to endure while we wrote the book. Thank you, Debbie for all of your love and support through the years.

Thank you to Denny Floden for hiring me, being my mentor, friend, and major contributor to Chapter 7 of the book. Without Denny Floden, there is no premeire "paying it forward" story, so essential to *Blind Vision*.

A special thanks for the insight of Joanna Wnuk, who gave us a kick in the rear, strongly recommending us to share more of the struggles and challenges in the book. She also helped capture special photographic moments of Chad and I. Her patience and commitment over the past two years is greatly appreciated while we worked on and finished the book.

Special gratitude for the careful insight and skillful suggestions of our publisher, Barbara Dee (especially while recovering from a near tragic car accident and helping us from the hospital room). This project took grit, patience and a lot of "coaching" from Barbara. Together we worked with her and the Suncoast Digital Press team, going over the book time and time again until it looked and felt right for the reader. Over the past two years, both Chad and I have grown to appreciate Barbara Dee not only as our editor and publisher, but as a person.

We acknowledge Jennie Harland Khan for her wonderful foreword and special insight as a transformational coach into my story, my life, and my son Chad's life.

Thank you to Dr. John Arden for being the first reviewer and for providing his scientific summary, included as Chapter 14 in our book. His special insight into the world of neuro-psychology explains how I (my brain) evolved through my tragedy, and how anyone can change their life, by changing their mind.

Thank you to Jennifer Grisanti, Bobby Crim, The Crim Foundation, Dr. Omprakash Sawlani, Mark Lowis, and Col. Nathan Miller for their wonderful endorsements.

Thank you to my friends and business associates who graciously shared how I have influenced them in some way. Our editor created an entire chapter (Chapter 13) from these heartfelt stories. Your friendships are what makes my life a little easier helping me forgot the darkness and see more of the light.

I want to thank all of my family for having the courage to allow me to tell our family's story, knowing it is difficult sharing the good, the bad, and the ugly with the whole world.

I want to thank my son, Chad, for writing this book for me, with me, and through me. The process has been deeply fulfilling.

Finally, I want to thank all veterans for their service and contributions to our country, to their fellow soldiers, and even more personally, for inspiring me to share my story. Know that you were in my mind and heart during the entire development of *Blind Vision*, and you still are.

—Howard Myers

Howard and Chad, Anna Maria Island, Florida (2018)

ABOUT THE AUTHORS

HOWARD MYERS is a motivational speaker, inspiring audiences from small church congregations to large conferences with thousands of attendees. He is the co-founder of Blind Vision, a company that provides coaching, workshops and training in personal empowerment. Non-profit organizations, veterans' groups, schools, churches and companies in multiple industries have asked Howard to bring his message of hope and empowerment to audiences from every walk of life.

Howard had a long career as "a multi-million dollar insurance producer who just so happens to be blind." Howard finished #2 in the nation among rookie agents as a career life insurance agent with Mass Mutual. Howard is a former national lives leader and winner of the Oscar of Salesmanship where he spoke to a crowd of 3,000 at Ford Theater with the late Paul Harvey.

Howard is published author, an inspirational speaker, a semi-retired independent insurance agent, co-founder of the Mindworks Performance Group, and along with his son, Chad, co-founder of Blind Vision. Howard may have lost his sight but never lost his vision.

He enjoys a very active lifestyle, residing in Michigan with his wife of 44 years, Debbie. He is a member of the Bobby Crim Hall of Fame, an avid runner, a family man, a father of four, and grandfather of seven.

CHAD MYERS is certified life coach, mentor, and inspirational speaker. His passion is to empower people to clarify their goals and achieve them. With his extensive background as a school teacher, he is able to make a profound difference in the lives of young people including aspiring athletes, those considering college, as well as those struggling teens who are in need of a strong role model and supportive mentor.

He has 25 years experience in the profession of education. He has worked with people from all walks of life from school aged children, to prison inmates, to corporate leaders. Chad is the co-founder of Blind Vision and also The Mindworks Performance Group.

Chad has a BS Ed. and M.Ed.; he attended University of Michigan, Michigan State University and Marygrove College. Chad is a proud parent of his 26-year-old son, Cameron, an advertising agency owner in Traverse City, MI. Chad and his fiancée, Joanna Wnuk, live on Long Boat Key in Florida.

Blind Vision complete! Howard and Chad,
Anna Maria Island (2018)

Made in the USA
Columbia, SC
18 March 2018